Elegance borne of brutality

Elegance borne of brutality
An eclectic history of the football boot

Ian McArthur and Dave Kemp

TWO HEADS
PUBLISHING

First published in 1995 by
Two Heads Publishing
9 Whitehall Park
London
N19 3TS

ISBN 1 897850 76 X

Photographs pages 29, 37, 43, 56, 72, 77 and in colour section – Allsport
Photograph page 70 and *Scifo* in colour section – Football Archive
Billy's Boots Copyright © Fleetway Editions, reproduced by kind permission

Cover and book design by Lance Bellers
Printed by Caldra House Ltd., Hove, Sussex
Bound by J W Braithwaite and Son Limited

We would like to thank all those people who helped and encouraged us through the various stages of this project. Special thanks to Audrey and Pat, and others close to us, who pretended to share our enthusiasm for this obsession.

We are particularly grateful to all the individuals and companies who sent us material and provided information on the fascinating world of football boots – specially to the team of three at Soccer Nostalgia and to Dave Williams at Puma UK.

Ian McArthur and Dave Kemp

The line up

Foreword

By Jim Gabriel

JIM GABRIEL BEGAN HIS illustrious career playing for Lawside Academy in his home town of Dundee. Spells with Tynecastle Boys and Dundee North End followed before he signed for Dundee FC in 1957.

Described by team-mate Doug Cowie (himself no slouch) as 'a natural', Jim's sharp and tenacious play, first as a centre half and then as a wing half, soon led to international recognition. He made his senior debut for Scotland in the Under-23 team against Wales in 1960, heralding the start of a short but effective Scotland career.

His decision to seek fame and fortune in the English league provoked a storm of protest amongst Dens Park fans when he moved to Everton for £30,000, giving an indication of the high regard in which he was held.

Further international honours, including full caps, followed during his 7-year spell with Everton. Thereafter he played for a series of English teams before deciding to lend his expertise and experience to the development of the game in the USA. He played for and coached Seattle Sounders for 5 years, and coached in Argentina, before returning eventually to Everton, where he continues to put much back into the game he obviously loves.

I WAS DELIGHTED TO BE ASKED BY DAVE AND IAN to write a foreword for their book. The selection of football boots has taken up a large part of my life, having started as a boot-wearing player at the tender age of six years until my retirement from playing at the age of thirty six. Even then I didn't 'hang up my boots', having been encouraged to step into the coaching and management part of football.

In all, I have been lacing up football boots for the best part of forty-eight years, during which time the boots have evolved from the once-dominant shape of the Manfield Hotspur to the slipper-like versions of today's 'wonder boots'. Now you can even buy a boot which puts more bend on your pass or shot, while I've been trying all this time to find a pair which can help me to hit the pass straight.

However, I do believe that when it comes to selecting football boots, then 'beauty is in the eye of the beholder', and to emphasise this point I will end with a short true story.

I was barely six years old when my dad presented me with my first pair of football boots. They were a beaten up, well-worn, hand-me-down pair of Manfield Hotspurs that the son of my dad's mate had outgrown. The boots must have been almost as old as I was and had certainly served more than one owner, yet when my dad handed them to me I was so proud and happy that I choked up and couldn't speak, not even to say "Thank you".

Instinctively I knew that my dad wasn't just giving me a worn down pair of Manfield Hotspurs; he was giving me a lift onto the first rung of the ladder of success, he was handing me a passport to travel the world playing football, he was presenting me with an opportunity to fulfil my boyhood dreams of winning League titles, Cup winners medals and International caps; he was giving me the tools I needed to practice and perfect my chosen trade.

Since that time I have worn many different types of football boots made by a variety of companies, all of whom have spent vast amounts of time and money researching, experimenting, discarding and finally unveiling their interpretation of the perfect pair of boots.

How could they know that my dad had handed them to me when I was just six years old?

Introduction

FOOTBALL BOOTS. LOVE THEM OR HATE THEM, you have to wear them if you're playing in a football match. And thousands of people do, week in, week out. Football is, after all, our national sport.

But why the fascination, and why devote a whole book to them?

It started with the Craig Johnston 'Predator' programme on T.V., when all of a sudden football boots were elevated to superstar status. Previously looked upon by Joe Public as mere objects with which you kicked a ball (or a player), boots were shown, in the space of half an hour, to be big business headline grabbers in their own right, regardless of who was wearing them. Boots, almost overnight, had class, glamour and charisma. Boots, in short, had arrived.

The sight of these £120-a-pair megastars certainly had a profound effect on us. Ian's thoughts were transported back through the mists of time to his youth, when he would lovingly clean his Stylo Matchmakers with a toothbrush after every game. That was fine, until his mother realised that he was using the same toothbrush to clean his teeth. The smartest guy in the team he may have been, but oh those green molars!

So we got thinking. If Ian had such vivid memories of early pairs of boots, then surely other football stars would as well. And when did all this boot business begin in the first place? What were boots like in the days of knickerbockers and shoulder charges? How on earth did they develop into the multi-million pound business that they are today?

We felt the story had to be told, and so set to work trying to unravel the history and mystery of these vital, but oft-overlooked, pieces of equipment. Early response to our letters was not encouraging - take, for example, our first reply, from the Football Association no less!

We were surprised and heartened by the fact that 2,000 books did not mention boots, and so Mr Barber's polite but negative epistle, in a perverse

kind of way, made us more determined than ever that the 2,001st book on his dusty shelves would deal with boots and nothing else!

We do not make claims for this book to be a definitive history of the football boot. We got waylaid, became bored with some areas, fascinated by others, so what you see before you is, in reality, more a celebration of the football boot, from pre-daters to Predators. There's historical stuff aplenty to keep any football buff satisfied; but there's more, much more than that.

And the title? Surprisingly enough, it's not meant to be as pretentious as it sounds, even though it is a line taken from a French poem (about boots, naturally).

Today's streamlined, smart and, yes, elegant boots are borne of the early primitive monstrosities which could maim, cripple or even kill. Since those days, the game has changed and developed in tandem with the type of footwear that has appeared on the market. A swerving free-kick from the edge of the box, perfected by the Brazilians and mimicked the world over thereafter, would not have been contemplated by a Manfield Hotspur wearer; he simply did not possess the tools to enable him to try it.

Total protection of all areas of the foot and ankle has been sacrificed for greater speed, greater control and greater feel of the ball, and who would argue that the game is not all the better for that? Managers and physios may complain that the incidence of ankle injuries is much higher these days, but by and large, players, and the game itself, have learned to adapt to the lighter footwear; there is no going back now. Show an old pair of Hotspurs to a young apprentice today and he will laugh out loud. Get him to try on a pair and he will be amazed that footballers ever managed to walk onto the pitch, let alone trail the boots around for 90 minutes, often in conditions which increased their already considerable weight two-fold.

So if there's no going back, the question ⟶

Dear Sirs,

Thank you for your letter of 13 May.

Our reference library here has 2,000 football books but virtually nothing on the boot. Perhaps the major manufacturers would have something, e. g. Mitre Sports, Bay Hall Works, Birkby, Huddersfield HD1 5AJ.

Are you sure there would be enough for a book?!

Sincerely

David Barber
Publications Office

must logically be – where do we go from here? We have tried to address this in the Extra Time section of the book, casting a whimsical eye towards the future. Perhaps in 100 years time, a follow-up book will be written, covering the 21st century and asking the same question. In it, managers may well express their regret at the passing of the rocket-powered, ostrich leather 'Aviator' boot, whilst at the same time giving thanks that Sunday morning physios tables are no longer cluttered with players suffering from 3rd degree burns.

Come with us, then, if you will. Check those studs one last time. Make sure those laces are nice and tight. Grab yourself a ball. Bounce it a couple of times if you're in the least bit nervous. Open the dressing room door, walk down the tunnel and salute the crowd. The game is about to begin.

This book is dedicated to David Barber in the Publications Office of the F.A. (which stands both for the Football Association and for the amount of information they have on boots) David - thanks.

WARNING: Whilst enjoying this book, resist the temptation to dig out your football boots past or present. You'll only want to touch, smell, or possibly even kiss them – hey, why not? Let's not be embarrassed about this. The memories connected to your boots are magical. Well, to you at least!

Along with every pass, tackle, chip and volley, who's been there with you? Yes, those boots; through the dream goal and the nightmare miss.

Cherish them, exalt them, even mount them on a marble plinth if you wish, but, above all, be grateful!

The warm up

THREE THINGS DRAW CROWDS OF WIDE-EYED, curious onlookers in school playgrounds:

1) A fight between two combatants which generally tells the onlooker to keep clear of the winner who, in all probability, is usually the school psycho-bully.

2) A pool of vomit, which informs the onlooker of a specific area of the playground to keep clear of. This is, of course, after inspecting it and deciding what delicious choice had been made at school dinners.

3) Someone showing off their new football boots, which can tell the onlooker a number of things; how spoilt or affluent the owner is; which footballer the proud owner idolises.

If we can assume that the crowds satisfy their natural curiosity for pecking order violence in number (1), and their lust for the unsavoury and squeamish in number (2), what attracts them to number (3), the new football boots? What makes them such an appealing draw? After all, the crowds don't gather when someone sports a new jumper or a new pair of shoes.

The following may be reasons why boots variably become the centre of attention.

a) They're worn by people we hero-worship.

b) We secretly desire to be those whom we hero-worship. →

SHORT PASS In the first set of rules drafted by the FA in the 1860s, No. 13 allowed a player to be kicked on the front of the leg whilst running with the ball – a practice known as 'hacking'.

13

c) We feel we can actually become our hero by intimating them; i.e. I wear the same boots as Ryan Giggs therefore I am Ryan Giggs.

d) This linkage to footballers we worship is somehow made concrete when we see 'their' boots in the flesh, or, more importantly, wear their boots on our flesh.

Has the football boot always held such curiosity value? How did the boot evolve from crude work boots into being today's stylised social barometers?

Association Football is, in its present form, a modern sport. As such, its history, apart from that of the boot, is well documented and its develop-ment is easy to trace. In some cases during the Middle Ages, it took the form of villagers squab-bling over a ball or, in extreme cases, the head of an executed Dane! Ouch! (wonder if this match-ball was sponsored by the local butcher?)

Football in those days was played in everyday footwear, was very robust, devoid of any rules, depended on brute force, and the philosophy of the survival of the fittest (obviously not any executed Dane) remained in play for about six centuries.

From the 14th Century onwards it was banned by seven monarchs; not because any of these royal figures couldn't do more than six at 'keepie-

The Crows' Feet Puzzle

BACK IN THE 1860s AND 70s, QUEENS PARK were regarded by many as the greatest team in the world. Formed in 1867, the amateurs from Glasgow possessed a record few could argue with. They did not lose a goal, let alone a match, until early 1875 against Vale of Leven, and conse-quently their 5th round Scottish Cup tie against Vale in the 1875/76 season was eagerly awaited. Queens Park were confi-dent, and desperate to avenge the defeat conceded the previous year. The stage was set for a classic.

The match was played on 30th December 1876. Hampden Park had been turned into a quagmire by constant rain which continued throughout the game, making life miserable for the 2,000 spectators who braved the elements.

Vale emerged 2-1 winners, a tragedy for Queens Park who had been beaten for the first time on their own ground, but the drama was by no means over. Queens Park officials inspected the pitch, and to their horror found great jagged marks on the sodden turf. There could be only one explanation – Vale players had been wearing spikes, thereby breaching Law 14 of the rules. The possibility that Queens Park players might have been responsible never entered into consideration, and it was decided that some form of action should be taken.

A two-man delegation was duly appointed to travel to Alexandria to investigate. They visited the homes of several Vale players and examined their boots with great care. No trace of spikes was discovered but still they remained convinced that the rules on footwear had been infringed. Irate Vale fans made claims that Queens Park supporters had deliberately marked the pitch with their umbrellas so that a protest could be engineered. "Perhaps crows made the marks", they added sarcastically.

Bitter letters were exchanged between the clubs. Queens Park were still adamant that "spikes had been worn by players belonging to one side or the other", and this refusal to retract the implication that Vale were guilty forced Vale eventually to complain to the Glasgow press; "it seems holes were discovered which, in the imagination of some charitable individuals, at once became spike marks. We now learn . . . that the holes had the appearance of having been made with umbrellas or walking sticks, as they varied in size. I can faithfully say the Vale of Leven team never played with spikes in their boots. This letter was not written through spite. We only want justice for I consider we have been shamefully used."

Spikes? Umbrellas? Crows' feet? Sharp-clawed aliens having a game of five-a-side? The mystery has never been solved.

SHORT PASS Rule No. 19 went even further on the subject of footwear, stating that 'no-one wearing projecting nails, iron plates or gutta percha on the sole of his boots is allowed to play'.

uppie', but because it was considered too dangerous, and was a threat to civilised society as well as interfering with such gentle pastimes as archery practice. In fact, the history of the game could be written in terms of how it was suppressed. All attempts to sink the boot into the game failed, however, and football, for all its fury, disorganisation and danger to limb and liberty (thankfully) just survived to be tamed and made respectable in the 19th Century.

The revival of football occurred in the public schools of England. Each school had its own set of rules, dependent mainly on the size of the ground available to play it on. Few schools had the large recreational area they possess nowadays, so the old, rough game of running with the ball and collaring was gradually replaced with a game where more skill with the use of the feet was required. More contact between foot and ball also meant that more consideration would be given to a type of footwear appropriate for play.

It was largely impossible for schools to play against one another, due to conflicting rules, and the opinion was that if a common code could be introduced, then regular sports could be played with other teams. Eventually this germ of an idea bore fruition in a meeting called between representatives of both Association and Rugby →

In the early days, the chances of a passing car interrupting a game of street football were remote.

clubs at the Freemason's Tavern, London on October 26th, 1863, during which a resolution was passed that the clubs represented be thereafter known as the FA. The elected secretary was asked to seek the opinions of the captains of the leading public schools, whilst at the same time a draft set of rules was drawn up, to be discussed at later meetings. Twenty-three rules were drafted in total, covering all aspects of the game. The rules are a mixture of present day rugby and football rules. Number 13, for example, allows for a player to be kicked on the front of the leg while running with the ball; a practice commonly known as 'hacking'. It is here, also, that the first attempt to

regulate the type of footwear worn is mentioned. Rule 19 states, "No-one wearing projecting nails, iron plates or gutta percha on the soles of his boots is allowed to play."

This was probably proposed by someone with painful memories of 'navvies' (special boots for hacking), described by a player from 1860 as having "a toe resembling the ram of an iron-clad." Players reproached for unnecessary violence would have their navvies removed and slippers substituted.

Meanwhile, the various schools met at Cambridge to formulate their rules, and it was the drawing up of these rules which eventually led to

See the advertisement, buy the boots, score a goal . . . easy.

Footwear manufacturers gradually developed boots especially for football.

Every boot was better, cheaper and more waterproof than its rival. Many claims were not as robust as the actual boots.

the split between the two sections, and resulted in the formation of the Association game on one hand, and the rugby code on the other.

The bone of contention centred around the question of the permissibility of hacking, and so obstinate were the two camps in their support for or dislike of this practice, that no compromise could be found. At a stormy meeting in December 1863 the supporters of hacking withdrew to form their own Rugby Union, and the game's future was left in the hands, or more appropriately, the feet, of those who had previously favoured the dribbling game. Consequently, all the rugby parts of the proposed rules were deleted. These rules,

the first set of Association Football laws of the game, were adopted on 8th December 1863 and again addressed the question of footwear; this time as the last of thirteen rules and left unchanged from the draft rules drawn up a couple of months previously.

It is important to know what came before and how various game styles evolved to become Association Football, or soccer. However, the real story of football is the story of great players great teams, great goals, great saves and . . . great BOOTS!

Forms of football footwear around the 1860s and 70s were any pair of leather boots or →

Stevens made the same boot for both football codes, with the added bonus of verbatim endorsements from leading players.

Not an early portent of white boots – Scotch Chrome was a new type of leather.

SHORT PASS All early boots were made with rock-solid toe-caps as all the kicking was done with the toe. Boots specifically designed and made for football were not introduced until the 1880s.

shoes that players possessed. Although most of these boots were lace-ups, some did have elasticated sides. These same boots would often double as workboots, or even, when cleaned and polished, treble as 'Sunday-best' boots. Such adaptability seems quite inconceivable when one considers the varieties of boots available for each and every leisure pursuit we participate in today.

Football at this time was a pastime of a handful of enthusiasts for whom the ball was the centre of attention and who scarcely gave a thought to the question of equipment.

The evolutionary process was, however, up and running, or rather plodding, when teams, leagues and competitions became established in the 1880s on a local, school and regional basis. From then on football boots slowly began to replace everyday boots on the feet of dedicated, sweat-encrusted men in municipal parks all over the country, to whom the Saturday game was everything. It emerged as part of the kit which also included heavy woollen shirts, thick stockings, and knickerbockers or long shorts.

Although there were some sportshoe manufacturers in existence, ordinary shoe and boot manufacturers considered it worthwhile to diversify into such a specialised area, indicating that the popularity of the game was magically

Boots and football 'knickers' slotted in conveniently with other sporting attire.

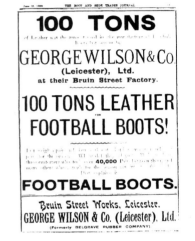

mushrooming, and more and more people were playing for kicks.

Shoe manufacturing heart and soul land, the East Midlands of England, along with main population centres such as London, Birmingham and Glasgow, provided numerous examples of leather boots made specifically for football.

Advertising material from the 1880s indicates that players had the choice of bars or studs, and in some cases could even specify any pattern they required.

So even though the game was becoming more widely played, manufacturers were keen to bow to the individual requirements of the customer.

Either that, or they did not know which was best. Early days indeed, and rather refreshing when you consider that nowadays all manufacturers claim that they know best!

The Premier football boots made by Mercer and Co. of Bolton are an early example of style overcoming practicality. With two-tone brogue appearance, strap and buckle, they do, as Hugh McIntyre's testimony suggests, look good enough to play football themselves without any assistance. For such a rugged sport, however, they do appear quite dandyish. The fact that Blackburn were one of the top teams of the day suggests that they compared favourably with competitors. →

THE "PREMIER" FOOTBALL BOOTS, 10s. 6d., 12s. 6d., & 14s. 6d.

HUGH M'INTYRE (Blackburn Rovers) writes—"The BOOTS are Splendidly Made and look Good Enough to play Football them-"selves without any assistance."

MERCER & CO.,
SOLE MANUFACTURERS,
64 TOWN HALL SQUARE,
BOLTON.

SOLD BY FIRST-CLASS DEALERS EVERYWHERE AT ONE UNIFORM PRICE.

A leading Blackburn player of the day was clearly happy to let his boots do the talking (and playing).

Early shin pads (made from canvas or leather) were no match for rock-solid toe-caps.

FOOTBALL OUTFITS.

WRITE FOR PRICE LIST.

CHEAPEST HOUSE IN THE TRADE.

A. W. GAMAGE
ATHLETIC OUTFITTER,
126, 127, 128, 129, HOLBORN, E.C.

A. W. GAMAGE,
126 to 129, HOLBORN, LONDON, E.C.

SHORT PASS Studs or bars attached to the sole of the boot were not standardised until 1891. Until this time, players were free to use whatever they wanted to find some traction – bits of horeshoe and blocks of wood were common additions.

Although some early adverts claimed lightness and pliability, compared with today's superlight, sophisticated, sleekline, logo-festooned slippers they were clumsy, armoured clodhoppers that reached above the ankle and weighed a ton. They did seem to suit (or rather dictate) the playing style of the time, which was undoubtedly more physical and less skilful than the game of today. (Depending on which team you support!)

The 'Stevens' patent Rugby and Association football boot was one of the brand leaders during

this time, and it is clear that they were keen to inform footballers that attention was being given by equipment manufacturers to the prevention of injuries to players of both codes. The toe-caps in particular come in for special mention. The harder the better, as at this time it was the norm to kick the ball with the toe, and boots were therefore made with rock-solid toe-caps which would protect the kicker's foot. What from? Another kicker's foot! Let's not forget also that a ball, especially a rain-sodden one, could weigh a fair amount, so it's

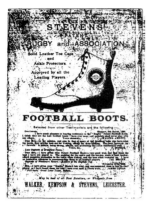

Stevens held firm with their ankle protectors and player testimonials.

Professionalism

ALTHOUGH PROFESSIONALISM was not legalized until 1885, many players before then received some form of remuneration for their efforts. The History of Ardwick states that wages were left inside players' ordinary boots, to be found when they dressed after the match.

The introduction of professionalism led to a rift developing in England between teams from the north and those from the south of the country. The northerners took to it like ducks to water, but the southerners resisted, with the result that northern teams enjoyed complete ascendancy over their southern counterparts for many years thereafter. So complete was their domination that teams from the south campaigned eventually for an amateur cup, which was duly introduced in 1893.

The term 'amateur' in those days was much more meaningful than it is today. Clubs found it increasingly difficult to field a team which was truly amateur in status. Players had to make long, expensive journeys and take time off work, so it was little wonder that players were

'assisted' in different ways. Another problem arose from the constant interchange of clubs by players. If a player was dropped by a particular team, he would simply try to get a game for another team that afternoon.

At the time, one of the Fulham players was a nippy left-winger by the name of Ernie Payne. He had been unable to get into the first team during the 1892/93 season, and was naturally becoming more and more disgruntled. Tottenham Hotspur, (amateur then, as were Fulham), offered him a game early in the next season, and he immediately accepted.

His first game for them was to be on the 21st of October, but when he went down to Fulham on the morning of the match to collect his gear, he found that the whole lot had been stolen. He hurried over to Tottenham to tell them what had happened. The club found him a pair of knickers and a shirt without any problem, but they could not provide him with a pair of boots, so he was given a ten-shilling note and told to buy a pair for himself. This he did, and he wore the

boots that afternoon.

However, officials of Fulham found out about the boots and, annoyed with the way a player had been snatched from under their noses, they lodged a complaint with the London FA, accusing Spurs of 'professionalism'.

On the 1st November, 1893 the Council of the London FA reported back their findings. They found Spurs in breach of Rule 10, stating that the payment given to Payne to buy boots was an unfair inducement offered to him to play for the club.

Tottenham appealed, stating that Payne had not actually been given the boots, and that it was understood that they remained the property of the club. Should he leave, he would not be permitted to take the boots with him. The appeal fell on deaf ears, however. Tottenham were suspended for two weeks, and although Payne went as far as to give the club back the ten bob, he received a one week suspension for his pains.

The Harrow side of 1867 were so ahead of the times, in sartorial terms, that they were wearing 'Chelsea boots' one hundred years before anyone else.

SHORT PASS Proving that some things never change in football, in 1893 Tottenham Hotspur were found guilty by the FA of making an improper payment to a player.

no wonder that the strength of the toe area was of prime importance.

The ankle protector was also highlighted and, for obvious reasons, it was appreciated by players of the time. Nowadays it is often difficult to separate fact from fiction when boot advertisements make claims to have gone beyond the bounds of perfection with some new innovation. However, in the 1880s when boots, purpose-built for football, were advertised, it was often obvious to see the benefits from injury-protecting innova-

tions such as the heel protector.

Another development of the time is that of a strap which crossed over the bottom two or three rows of eyelets, widening to the outside of the foot. This was presumably a strengthener for the striking area, and also to protect an area which could come in contact with the ball when shooting.

An aspect of boot manufacturing in the 1880s which is worth noting involves testimonials from some of the great players of the time. After all, if you've got Wattie Arnott, the Scottish super- $\longrightarrow$

star of the time, saying he won't play in any other pair, then they must be the best. Testimonials from players as far afield as America and New Zealand suggest that football was becoming increasingly popular in different parts of the world, and wherever there were footballers, then of course boots would be required. After all, an ankle needs protection in any language!

In 1891 it was decided that standardised leather studs or bars on the heels or the sides of the boots would be allowed. Manufacturers had previously anticipated this decision as they had

been listening to what the players were saying, and they'd therefore been making and advertising these boots a few years prior to the ruling coming into effect. Players running at pace, turning on a florin and shooting for goal could now legally 'keep their feet', (which seemed reasonable, as they belonged to them anyway) on muddy, slippery and uneven surfaces. It would be pleasing to think that allowing players to wear protrusions on the heels and soles of their boots came about through an increased sophistication in the game where boots were looked upon as tools as $\longrightarrow$

The British Ladies Football Club plays its first match, in 1895, with a 'ringer' for goalkeeper.

Tottenham, never slow to grasp the commercial nettle, hosted a match in 1914 played by The Theatrical Ladies' Football Team.

opposed to weapons. The reality was, however, that this legalising of studs and bars was a way of standardising what was seen by the authorities as a problem. Players keen to stay vertical during a game had, for some time, been buying boots with studs or bars, or hammering in their own form of traction, which included anything from bits of horseshoe to small blocks of wood. The ruling body had acted through necessity, albeit belatedly, (but then, what's new?). The FA had to be seen to have more of a grip on the game than those players who sported studs or bars had when playing, and this grip was tightened when the stud was further regulated to be a plug built up of layers of leather; a ruling which stood up until the 1940s.

To protect players and eliminate any devious doctoring of studs or bars by a small minority of scallywags, referees were authorised in 1900 to examine players' boots before a match; a practice still carried out today in both the amateur and professional game.

In the 1890s manufacturers were eager for a larger share in the market, as they were now used to the idea that football was not just a fad. They were now assured of its permanence and aware that the numbers playing the game were growing.

Adverts of this time now boasted boots being made in scotch chrome. A new form of mineral tannage had been introduced in 1884 when chromium salts were used for the first time. Chrome tanning, as it developed, resulted in such leathers as box calf, which was strong, supple and highly water resistant, and therefore used for footwear uppers. As well as durability being a marketable factor, stylishness of the upper is also mentioned, which suggests that the boot now also had to be aesthetically pleasing. Although the adverts from this period still boast the hardness of the toe, the innovation of the rubber in-step pad in the latest Stevens boot suggests that parts of the boot other than the toe were contributing to actual play and were used for striking the ball. The fact that it doubles as a protector is an added selling point.

OK – we've warmed up. Now it's time for the first half . . .

SHORT PASS Specific rules on football boots, regulating all aspects of the technical specification and appearance, remained in the laws of the game until 1990 when simplicity ruled at last. Current regulations state 'A player shall not wear anything which is dangerous to other players.'

The first half

BY 1900 FOOTBALL WAS GROWING UP AND WAS becoming the game of the people. The evolution of the boot was also gathering pace, albeit that of a snail. New materials were available and more people were playing the game.

Frank Sugg boots were worn by Liverpool and Everton players at the turn of the century, and although they still cover high over the ankle, the toe is still of iron-hard leather, and they're still as pliable as concrete, these boots at least appear to have slightly smaller heels and threaten to develop a style of their own.

During the first decade of the 20th Century progress was slow but there developed a wider choice available in types of leather and range of colour. Many general footwear manufacturers, eager to join in on the game, now devoted a whole page to football boots. A white, velvet chrome boot made by Barratts in 1905 suggests that players wishing to stand out from the crowd could now strut their studs in style!

New innovations are also appearing, such as the 'Torpedo Toe' and the 'Waist Brace' (how we wish we had pictures of those!).

Such changes would appear to indicate that there was a degree of consultation going on between manufacturers and exponents of the game, regarding comfort and suitability for $\longrightarrow$

SHORT PASS In 1901 the maximum wage for a professional footballer was £4 per week.

25

Borrowed Boots

As a schoolboy football-fanatic of the wartime '40s, life was made very difficult owing to the lack of availability of football gear.

Jerseys were no problem; any old shirt or vest would do. As for shorts - well, we wore shorts to school every day anyway. Socks could be anything long enough to hold the Reader's Digest or the like as shin guards.

Football boots, however, were a distinct luxury, especially to someone who depended on only a few pence every week to see him through. On occasions, however, I found the answer to my problem – my older brother. He was the proud possessor of a real pair of football boots, as he played for the local XI.

Fortunately for me he was employed in the local cinema as a projectionist, which entailed working Saturday afternoons – ample opportunity for me to make use of his boots when he was otherwise engaged. On most days a quick clean up, a couple of studs renewed and a quick polish concealed my crime.

The first pair of boots that I owned was actually half a pair (the right one), as my brother, who was fortunately left-footed, owned the other. We had come to an agreement, settled by our mother, that each would wear one of the boots whilst wearing an ordinary shoe on the other!
— *Gordon Andrews*

play. It is also apparent that some manufacturers, for example Joseph Leeson and Sons Ltd. of Leicester, saw the Rugby and Association version as a similar game which, although was not the case, did widen their selling potential for one product; lazy but perhaps a sensible approach.

The Frank Sugg collection of 1905 clearly demonstrates an ever-increasing amount of eager and discerning customers. It is also obvious that consideration has gone into countering the various difficult playing conditions; rubber bars for frosty weather and 'Frost Boots' with felt soles which were considered "a very good idea for playing on hard ground" by J. Beveridge of Millwall FC.

The 'Forward Boot', sporting (or rather unsporting) a heel and with lacing that travels close to the toe suggests that the position it was named after was a specialist one, requiring specialist equipment; at least, this is what the manufacturers wanted the public to believe.

An aspect of these times which must have had manufacturers rubbing their hands with glee was that games periods had become an officially sanctioned part of the school curriculum in British state elementary schools (those were the days). Manufacturers offered boots in boys' sizes at

Liverpool and Everton players were running around wearing boots like these in the 1900s.

FRANK SUGG

32 Lord Street, LIVERPOOL.

The Special Chrome, Laced to Toe, Cane Waist, Permanent Indestructible Block Toe.

6/

POST FREE.

Warranted Waterproof, Post Free, 6/.

Can only be procured from the Maker—

FRANK SUGG, LIVERPOOL.

Write for Illustrated Catalogue, all Requisites, Post ree.

SHORT PASS In the early 1900s, a leading Northampton footwear manufacturer called Manfield introduced the now legendary 'Manfield Hotspur', endorsed by Spurs. By the mid-1920s, 100,000 players were using Hotspurs.

slightly reduced prices, and although they sold well enough to justify inclusion in catalogue ranges, younger footballers would more likely be the recipients of well-worn hand-me-downs, with toes stuffed with newspaper.

A company that ranked alongside Suggs as one of the market leaders was Shillcocks of Birmingham, whose renown had exploded into the top corners of many people's minds during the last decade of the previous century. Aston Villa, who had won the FA Cup in 1895 wearing Shillcock boots, allowed the trophy to be centre-piece of a shop window display. This would obviously have attracted boot buyers, but unfortunately it also attracted the attention of thieves who proceeded to steal it!

Indeed, by 1910, Shillcock's genuine McGregor, named after the founder of the football league, (a clever association that perhaps suggested his approval), became a huge seller with amateurs and professionals at home and abroad. Professional patronisation of the company obviously influenced the orders from amateurs.

Shillcock stressed the importance of choosing quality boots (no doubt those made at his factory) by stating "Given two teams of equal calibre, →

Broken in

In the 1908 FA Cup final between Wolves and Newcastle, the Wolves centre-forward George Hedley played in a pair of battered, well-patched boots. Later in the game the boots were in such a bad condition that they were hanging off his feet. The trainer tried to get him to put on a new pair, but Hedley refused, preferring to keep them on rather than suffer the trauma of playing in a pair which had not been broken in.

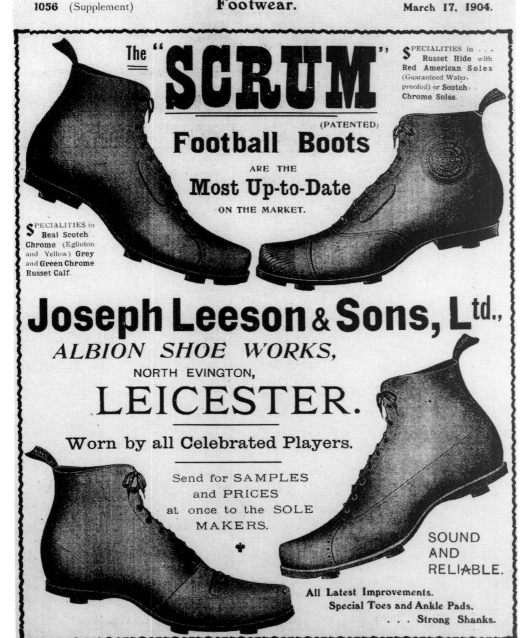

The same boots were deemed suitable for Association Football and Rugby Football by many makers.

victory would probably go to the better shod team." Horses for courses.

He was, of course, correct and his factory provided non-gimmicky boots that appeared to meet the demands of many thousands of footballers. His factory around 1905 was state of the art. The very latest lasting machines, imported from America and described as practically a steel pair of hands capable of gripping, clutching and pulling the upper, worked alongside English-made presses used for cutting components such as the sole, heel and toe stiffeners. Other machines included a stud-making machine which drove

rivets through three plates of leather, leaving the stud ready for fitting in one operation. A sole-levelling machine and eye-letting machine completed the process. It must be remembered, however, that the judgement and skill of the workman was invaluable, especially in cutting leather of uniform thickness for the tops, and of course in operating the machinery.

A boot whose fame rose to the top of the division was the Manfield Hotspur. Up until 1904, Manfield, a leading Northampton footwear company, had recorded sales of boots on a par with other manufacturers. Then the Hotspur was

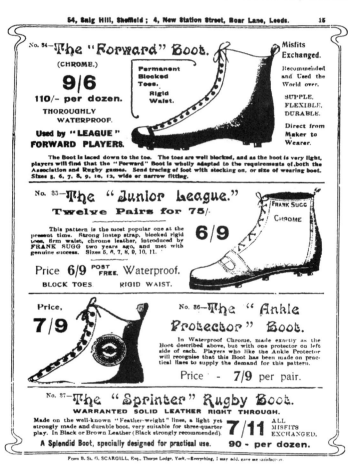

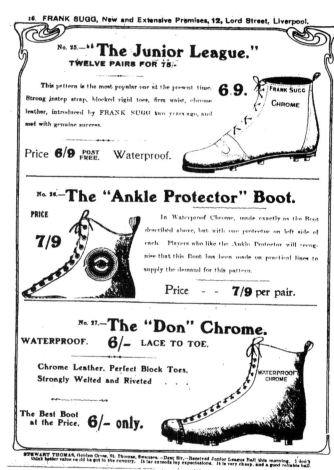

Endorsements aren't what they used to be – Mr Scargill of York was pleased to say "Everything, I may add, gave me satisfaction".

Mr Thomas of Swansea was even more fulsome after receiving his Junior League Ball – "It far exceeds my expectations".

SHORT PASS In 1922, W. Abbott and Sons Ltd. produced an early Predator by introducing rows of stitching across the toe "to ensure accurate kick direction" and improve control over the ball.

produced, which turned the tide completely, with sales surpassing even the 'Embekay' made in Kettering and the 'McGregor', both products of exclusive boot-makers.

Tottenham Hotspur adopted it, giving Manfield permission to use their famous name on it, and it was well on its way to becoming a star – along with another boot made by a rival Northampton company, Read, Myall and Read, also known as the Hotspur. And who endorsed this rival boot? None other than Tottenham Hotspur, who one can only imagine distributed their favours lavishly!

Because of this clashing of registrations and subsequent court proceedings, the Manfield version had to be prefixed to become 'Manfield Hotspur' around 1915, with the Read, Myall and Read version then being promoted as the 'Genuine Hotspur', obviously suggesting that it was the real thing, sort of.

Both Northampton companies made excellent boots, and indeed their intense rivalry meant they had to utilise every opportunity in their advertising literature to kick home how their own version was superior. Association with name players and cup-winning sides was part of the 'our boots are better than anyone elses' approach. →

Borrowed Boots

Tommy Docherty is described in his biography as "the teenager from the slums of Glasgow who had survived on handouts and borrowed football boots"

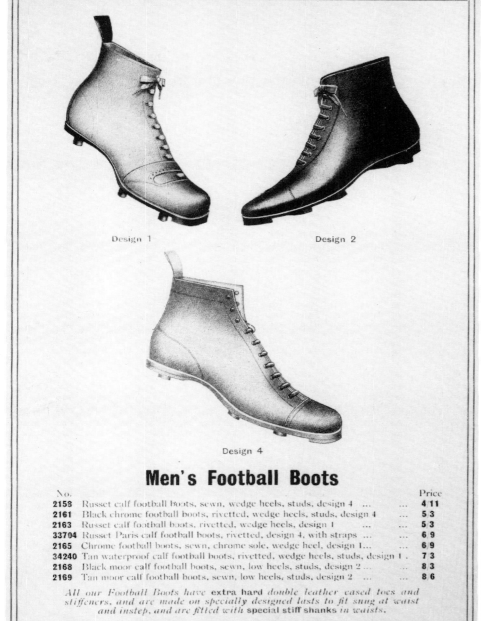

Design 1   Design 2

Design 4

Men's Football Boots

No.		Price
2158	Russet calf football boots, sewn, wedge heels, studs, design 4	4 11
2161	Black chrome football boots, rivetted, wedge heels, studs, design 4 ...	5 3
2163	Russet calf football boots, rivetted, wedge heels, design 1	5 3
33794	Russet Paris calf football boots, rivetted, design 4, with straps ...	6 9
2165	Chrome football boots, sewn, chrome sole, wedge heel, design 1... ...	6 9
34240	Tan waterproof calf football boots, rivetted, wedge heels, studs, design 1 .	7 3
2168	Black moor calf football boots, sewn, low heels, studs, design 2 ...	8 3
2169	Tan moor calf football boots, sewn, low heels, studs, design 2 ...	8 6

All our Football Boots have **extra hard** *double leather cased toes and stiffeners, and are made on specially designed lasts to fit snug at waist and instep, and are fitted with* **special stiff shanks** *in waists.*

With Stevens' boots, wipe off the mud, remove the studs and bars, and you're ready for a night out.

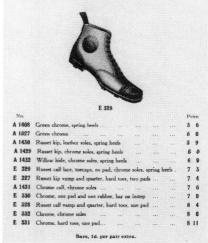

Football Boots.

E 328

No.		Price
A 1408	Green chrome, spring heels	5 6
A 1627	Green chrome	5 0
A 1430	Russet kip, leather soles, spring heels	5 9
A 1429	Russet kip, chrome soles, spring heels	5 0
A 1432	Willow hide, chrome soles, spring heels	6 9
E 329	Russet calf lace, toecaps, no pad, chrome soles, spring heels .	7 3
E 327	Russet kip vamp and quarter, hard toes, two pads	7 4
A 1431	Chrome calf, chrome soles	7 6
E 330	Chrome, one pad and one rubber, bar on instep	7 9
E 328	Russet calf vamp and quarter, hard toes, one pad	8 4
E 332	Chrome, chrome soles	8 6
E 331	Chrome, hard toes, one pad...	8 11

Bars, 1d. per pair extra.

Oddballs

Some of the greatest eccentrics have been the brave few who decided that the best way to stand out was to not wear boots at all. Come on down, Abdul Salim, a trialist signed by Celtic in the 1930s who refused to wear boots, playing instead with bandages on his feet. In the days of the Manfield Hotspur, this was asking for trouble, the sporting equivalent of a fireman entering a blazing warehouse wearing a shellsuit and sneakers. And what was Abdul Salim doing in Glasgow in 1936? Simple, he was a seaman, and his boat was docked there for a while.

Manfield's were not slow to promote player and team association and their 1910 range clearly demonstrates this, but another aspect that is perhaps more interesting is the use of a detachable heel-grip – a device used to aid grip of the heel. Leather in use game after game, season after season, (up to 6, 7 or 8 was not uncommon), would loosen and thus afford less grip, presumably resulting in the player's foot doing its best to leap out of the boot every time he kicked the ball. The heel-grip was designed to counteract this. Perhaps this is where the bawled instruction from coach to player, 'Come on lads, get a grip!' came from.

A surprising aspect in these heady days of increased output and mechanisation in the footwear industry was the fact that the world-beating Manfield Hotspur was assembled by hand. Octogenarian Alfred Rayson of Northampton, →

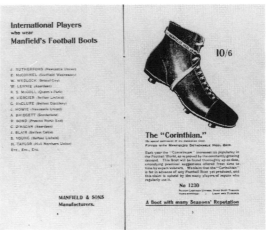

Manfield were keen to include the 'detachable heel grip' on all their leading models.

At this time, in-depth technical detail was more important than aesthetics.

Manufacturers quickly moved from supplying individual players to meeting the needs of the whole team.

Famous Clubs
supplied with
Manfield's Football Boots

NEWCASTLE UNITED
ABERDEEN
BELFAST DISTILLERY
MIDDLESBROUGH
BROUGHTON RANGERS
SWINTON
BRISTOL CITY
MANCHESTER CITY
SUNDERLAND
HUDDERSFIELD
SALFORD
BRADFORD CITY
DUNDEE
ARBROATH
BRADFORD PARK AVENUE
HULL
DUBLIN BOHEMIANS
ETC., ETC.

MANFIELD & SONS
Manufacturers.

10/6

The "HOTSPUR"

(By permission of the Directors of the Tottenham Hotspur Club)

Our object has been to make this boot one of great strength and durability at all points. Its rounded sole (without projecting edges) avoids clogging, and therefore gives to the wearer a distinct advantage when playing on heavy ground. This feature is not experimental, but one of practical utility, and its value is endorsed by the approval of all who have worn the boot

No. 1235

SMOOTH RUSSET HIDE, HARD BUTT TOECAPS, FITTED WITH MANFIELD'S DETACHABLE HEEL GRIP.

SPECIAL FEATURE—ROUNDED SOLE, NO HEEL OR WELT

SHORT PASS Read, Myall and Read of Northampton registered the word Hotspur as a trademark in 1894 and in a subsequent battle with Manfield claimed to be a supplier of football boots to Spurs from as far back as 1885.

Worn by
100,000
players.

"THE **Manfield** Hotspur"

1. Solid butt **toe**, non-kinking.
2. Rounded sole to edge prevents mud-clogging and smartens action.
3. Waist arch of strength and spring.
4. Bevel-edged stiffener fits snugly and protects heel.
5. Hand-curried Russet Butt Leather, waterproof and supple, as used in no other boot.
6. Lock-rivetted studs, placed **for** most grip and support.

AS PROOF OF ITS SUCCESS, the MANFIELD-HOTSPUR is the most imitated Football Boot ever made.

As WITNESS TO ITS SUPREMACY, it is the chosen boot of the principal clubs of the world, whose players are surely judges of the BEST!

PRICE 20/-
from 59 & 60, ST. PAUL'S CHURCHYARD, **E.C.**4 or any Manfield Branch or Agency.

Manfield
& SONS LTD

FREE KICK

Abdul Salim made a name for himself in the 30s with the barefooted look, but playing without boots caused a bit of a rumpus at the 1950 World Cup finals. The Indian team, who had qualified for the first time, were withdrawn from the tournament after being refused permission to play without boots.

one of the few remaining people who worked at Manfield pre-1940, recalls that after the various parts of the boot had been made at the main factory in Northampton, they were then picked up by good old Mr Starmer in a horse and cart. He would take the 12 lots to the county depot at Harpole, 5 miles away, where they would then be sewn together by hand. On return to the factory they would be inspected to see if they were up to the standard required. Assuming perfection, they would be boxed and distributed to awaiting footballers' feet throughout the world.

There appeared to be no gimmicky innovations surrounding this boot; no 'torpedo toe', no 'rubber instep pad', not even a choice of colour, but it sold and sold like no other boot that had kicked a ball before. Quality and value for money seem to have been the reasons for its popularity. By the mid 1920s, 80% of British teams and one hundred thousand players in other parts of the world were wearers. They could even boast that they helped the war effort; converting the factory to produce military materials – football boots were adapted to become officers' boots.

Clearly most football boots from 1910 to 1940 were based on the design features of the Hotspur, but innovators were still striving for their own version of the perfect boot. →

Hotspur
(Trade Mark Registered 1894)

THAT word and that alone is, and has been for thirty years our Registered Trade Mark (infringers will be proceeded against), and "Hotspur" is all the player need ask for when he requires the best possible in Football Boots.

"Hotspur" Football Boots were supplied by us to the "Spurs" team as far back as 1885, and in 1894 we registered the WORD "Hotspur," after a test of nearly forty years, re-registering it in 1908 and again in 1922.

We have no need to prefix our name to the word "Hotspur." It stands alone and its position is unassailable for Quality, Value and Endurance.

BEWARE OF SPURIOUS IMITATIONS.

Year by year players are becoming more and more discerning and careful in their purchases of Football Boots. They have seen imitations, sold perhaps under a similar name, and may be have been persuaded to try a pair of these so-called "almost as good" boots. But the player who does so very soon regrets it. In a way this sort of thing helps us, for it proves to the player by his own experience that the Genuine "Hotspur" is the best and cheapest in the long run, and he will not try any more "just as good" imitations, but will stick always to the GENUINE "HOTSPUR" REGISTERED FOOTBALL BOOTS

The signs by which discriminating players may identify the Genuine "Hotspurs."
1 The perforation of the words "Hotspur Regd." on outside Upper of every boot.
2 The "Nulli Secundus" device which together with "Hotspur Regd." is stamped on every sole.
3 The impression of the Makers' name "Read, Myall & Read, Northampton," on every sole and inside every upper.
Look for these signs and refuse any boots that do not show them.
Our success as Football Boot Makers to the English Cup Winners is unrivalled.

Alfred Rayson worked at Manfield's in the days when boots were moved around by horse and cart.

GENUINE "HOTSPUR" SUNDRIES

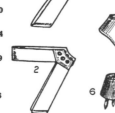

No.		per pair s. d.
1	Plain Leather Ankle Grip, without fittings with laces ...	1 0
2	Non-stretch Webbing Ankle Grip, Leather fittings, with laces ...	1 0
2a	Leather Ankle Grip with Leather fittings, with laces	1 4
3	Leather Hockey boot Ankle Grip, padded, with laces	1 9
5	Leather Hockey boot Ankle Grip, fitted with "Aerolite" Pneumatic Rubber Pads, with laces ...	2 6
4	Football Boot Bars, complete with nails as shown per set	0 9
6	Conical Studs for Rugby boots per set	0 4
7	Best quality Association Studs per set	0 3
8	Butt Leather Shin Guard, well padded per pair	2 6
9	Butt Leather Shin Guard, well padded, large size, for Professionals per pair	3 6

SOLE MANUFACTURERS:
Read, Myall & Read
NORTHAMPTON
ENGLAND

Every one of these unlikely looking extras was designed to fit the Read, Myall and Read Hotspur.

Broken in

My dad was a junior footballer in the 20s and 30s. He played for Coats Juniors, who were attached to the thread mills in my home town of Paisley.

When he bought a new pair of boots which were all leather, he would put them on his feet with no socks on, then steep his feet in a bath of water. The boots would shrink into the shape of his feet.

He always looked after them as if they were made of gold. He cleaned them after every match. He would dubbin them after they had been cleaned and aired out, and he always had spare studs and laces, just in case.

— *Mrs Agnes Jones, Shropshire*

It was the 'Nulli Secundus' device (see middle left) which distinguished a 'genuine' Hotspur from a mere Hotspur.

Borrowed Boots

Sir Matt Busby had a memory of his boyhood hero, Alex James. As a teenager James played for Old Orbiston Celtic when Matt was the team's hamper boy. One day, when James' boots got lost, Matt solved the problem by racing the two hundred yards to his home to fetch his own – they were a perfect fit for the little genius.

The 'Abbo' boot from 1920 boasted a non-skid toe which allegedly prevented the ball from skidding or slicing from the boot in the wet or mud. How was this remarkable claim achieved? By rows of stitching across the toes! Simple, wasn't it? West Ham United player Sydney Puddefoot, known as 'Our Syd', loudly endorsed this startling innovation. Not content though, W. Abbot and Sons improved on this, and by 1922 more rows of stitching criss-crossed the original to ensure accurate kick direction.

Boots made by Shillcock of Birmingham featured 'the only perfect ankle grip', which was an integral part of the boot's design as opposed to

the detachable version offered by rivals. By now, though, many players did not bother with purpose-built grips, but instead tied longer laces around the waist and then around the ankle through a leather loop, which served the same purpose.

The ankle area obviously still provided a vulnerable point, and ways of making this area more comfortable included wearing an additional pair of socks or strapping up with bandages.

A boot similar in design to its competitors was the 'Fanny Walden Kupwinna'. If you were one of a group of players boasting about your football boots, it would be okay to say "I've got a pair of

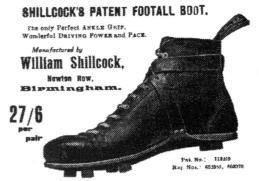

Makers battled to produce a device which would prevent the boot slipping off the heel.

The Progressive Boot Company never really broke through in the way Stylo Matchmakers would fifty years later.

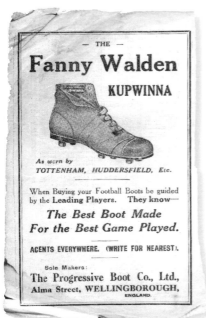

If you wore K-O football boots it didn't matter how badly you played – the boots won on their own!

Hotspurs" or "I've got a pair of Sugg's", but the boast concerning Fanny Waldens could easily be misconstrued! An advert from 1925 for Knock-Out boots demonstrates that the same boots are still used for the Rugby and Association codes, and that endorsement of players in Cup finals obviously continues to be an important selling-point. The boast, in this instance, is that Smith, Jack and Vizard wore them in the 1923 FA Cup final playing for Bolton Wanderers. They understandably fail to mention that the remainder of the Bolton team wore Hotspurs – that's the 'Genuine' variety; a point which Read, Myall and Read ram home in their 1924 catalogue, through a testi-

mony by Chas Foweraker, Bolton's manager. The same catalogue also contains an unsolicited testimony from Chas Paynter, trainer of West Ham United, the beaten finalists.

An entire page of the catalogue is devoted to a brief history of the boot, discriminating marks of identification, and a warning against spurious imitations sold perhaps under a similar name; wonder who they were referring to? Genuine Hotspur sundries are also on offer, including bars, studs and two varieties of ankle grip.

The 1927 catalogue boasts sales of over 100,000 pairs, endorsements by Arsenal and Cardiff City, and gives details of boots in the →

'Abbo' was the first 'Predator', with its unique toe-cap. The 'Kikeesi', with a double fortified toe, was aimed at goal-keepers and backs.

Hotspur range including the Popular, the Junior, The Featherweight and the special Professional.

Heels, although not available from all manufacturers, are still prevalent, but much smaller than those of 20 years previously.

A boast that these Hotspurs were also worn by Tottenham in the Cup final 6 years earlier suggests that Read, Myall and Read were hanging on to former glories. The following decade's domination by rivals Manfield clearly demonstrates that the popularity of the 'Genuine Hotspur' was on the wane.

By the mid 1930s, boots, although still of a familiar design, were changing slightly. The →

Oddballs

In the years before World War I, Herbert Chapman played in a distinctive pair of yellow boots. The rumours that he attracted the chant of "Ooh Aah ba-na-na!" wherever he played have however been proven to be historically inaccurate.

This is what the Wolverhampton Wanderers boot locker looked like in 1952.

The 'Futbalas' boot lace was so versatile it did the job of an ankle strap too.

NO ANKLE STRAPS NEEDED.

WON'T PULL NARROW

"FUTBALAS" FOOTBALL BOOT LACE.

From SPORTS OUTFITTERS, etc.

If any difficulty in obtaining write direct to

J. & W. EASTWOOD, Croft Mill, Whitefield, nr. Manchester.

ankle was still covered, but lacing was now through seven rows of eyelets as opposed to the 8-12 of a few years earlier. More often than not the top eyelets would not be laced so that the high sides were not too tight against the ankle, and the tongue would have freedom to drop forward, thus giving more room for flexibility. Players were now demonstrating, through their actions, exactly what they wanted.

The laws of the game were also changing, and in 1934 a law was passed whereby a player could actually be sent off and banned from playing if illegal footwear was used, only to be rescinded later by the FA. However this law was altered during the following year so that a player could be allowed back onto the field if the offending part of the footwear was adjusted. Usually this would mean obtrusive nails being hammered in to become flush with stud level.

Laws may have changed, but the emphasis was

Manfield's claimed that they received so many letters of thanks that it would be tedious to reproduce them.

"Soccer's Famous Boot" – and the 'only' boot according to Manfield.

SHORT PASS As leather studs wore down, it was not uncommon for protuding nails to be hammered flush with stud level during a game.

still on wearing good quality boots as opposed to fancy ones. Manfield, by way of genuine appreciation from amateur and pro alike, placed comprehensive advertising in the numerous football handbooks and marketed their boots through a wide range of retailers the length and breadth of Britain. They dominated the market and truly became, as one of their adverts boasted, 'The force behind the Football world'.

Their big three, the 'Hotspur', the 'United' and the 'Villa', each distinctive in its own right (e.g. the United had more of a heel than the Hotspur) were seemingly worn by everyone, everywhere and the manufacturers lost no time in telling this to the world.

It seemed that nothing could stop the Manfield conquering the world but alas, someone else had exactly the same idea and the 2nd World War meant issues more important than world-wide domination of the football boots market →

Oddballs

Len Shackleton, the Clown Prince of English football, made his debut for his country against Denmark in 1948 wearing a pair of rugby boots. "They're more comfortable", he explained, after being sent off for running with the ball and singing "Swing low, sweet chariot" in a deep baritone.

MANFIELD·HOTSPUR

MANFIELD·HOTSPUR
M
HANDMADE

The Boot of 1000 Cup Ties

Four widths.
Half-sizes.
(Relative prices, boys.)

18/9

Postage extra.

STRANGE that other good Football Boots have not risen to fame, isn't it? Strange, until you consider how comp'etely MANFIELD-HOTSPUR holds the field . . . got famous before others had a chance . . . and satisfies all expectations to-day. Everybody wears it, in all good matches all over the world.

MANFIELD & SONS, LTD.
107 Old Christchurch Road. Bournemouth.

What a boot! Less than £1 per pair and 1,000 Cup Ties too.

were now on the agenda – well, for the next five years at any rate.

Football boots production during war years was reduced drastically as army boots became the in-thing. However, football was still played at home and by the forces overseas, who were encouraged to keep up their fitness. Boots that were in stock were supplied to the troops who, perhaps for a few brief moments, could take their minds off the war by swivelling in the sand and tanking a shot into the net.

The post-war years saw an increase in competition for the established football boot manufacturers. J.W. Fosters and Sons were establishing themselves as a company with a sound reputation on the football field. Fosters boots were worn by professional clubs including Manchester United, Newcastle, Liverpool and Bolton. The entire Moscow Dynamo team, on a tour of the West designed to promote goodwill between two wartime allies, returned to the USSR with Fosters boots. The design, similar to other makes, was distinctly pre-war, but war itself and the necessity to improvise and innovate with new materials, meant that the shape of things to come would be very different.

SHORT PASS The Timpson K–O 'Knock-Out' boot was worn in the 1923 FA Cup Final by Bolton Wanderers and also in the 1924 Rugby Challenge Cup final by Oldham Rugby Club.

Half time

IN 1948, SOUTHAMPTON FC TOURED BRAZIL AT THE invitation of Botofogo FC, who are based in Rio. Football in Brazil at that time was well on its way to being the national institution it has now become, thanks mainly to the influence of Charles Miller, a fascinating character who is widely regarded as the father of Brazilian football.

Born in Brazil of British parents, Miller worked for the Sao Paulo Railway company when he set about encouraging the employees of British-owned firms to start playing the game. When Miller arrived home in his native Sao Paulo in 1894 after 10 years of education in England, he discovered football was virtually unknown there. A decade later, he could boast in his old school magazine that there were up to 60 clubs in Sao Paulo alone, attracting as many as 3,000 spectators to league games. Nearly every village had a club by this time, and over 2,000 footballs had been sold in a year.

It was not only his love of football which caught the imagination of the Brazilians. In 1990, Sao Paulo's English-language magazine *Village Voice* recalled, ". . . he won fame for his dribbling skills. He developed the trick of kicking the ball with his heel, and thus this move became known in Portuguese as a 'Charlie', later corrupted to 'Chaleira', the Portuguese for kettle." Perhaps, then, his love of the game and style of →

SHORT PASS Brazil were responsible for launching the lightweight boot revolution in England. Sir Stanley Matthews acquired a pair of the Brazilian footwear after watching them play in the 1950 World Cup and asked the Co-op in England to copy them!

 41

football left an impression on the Brazilians.

To the Southampton team who disembarked from the cruiser at Rio, this must have been like stepping into a totally alien world altogether. Their first game, against Fluminese in Rio, was played under floodlights, a first for the team, but it was the difference in footwear between the two teams which was the biggest eye-opener. Ted Bates, former manager of Southampton FC and a member of the tour party, recalls that the Brazilians wore very light, soft leather boots, "almost like slippers", whilst the English boots were of heavy leather with solid black toes. As far as the mobility of the respective teams were concerned, it

reminded him of the difference between carthorses and racehorses.

Dazzled by the floodlights, and outpaced by the light-footed Brazilians, Southampton went down 4 - 0 in what was a soccer education in more ways than one.

Two years after the Southampton tour, the England national side was in Brazil for the 1950 World Cup finals. Stanley Matthews was one of the players who went along to watch the opening game, and he recalls watching in amazement at what the Brazilians were doing on the pitch. Not only did the lightness of their footwear give them increased speed; the suppleness of the $\longrightarrow$

The fastest, the best, and also the most forward-thinking when it came to football boots.

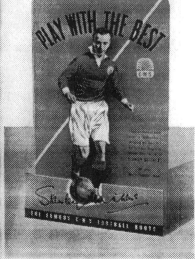

Sir Stanley Matthews finally hangs up his boots.

SHORT PASS Stanley Matthews received £20 per week from CWS for boot sponsorship in 1950.

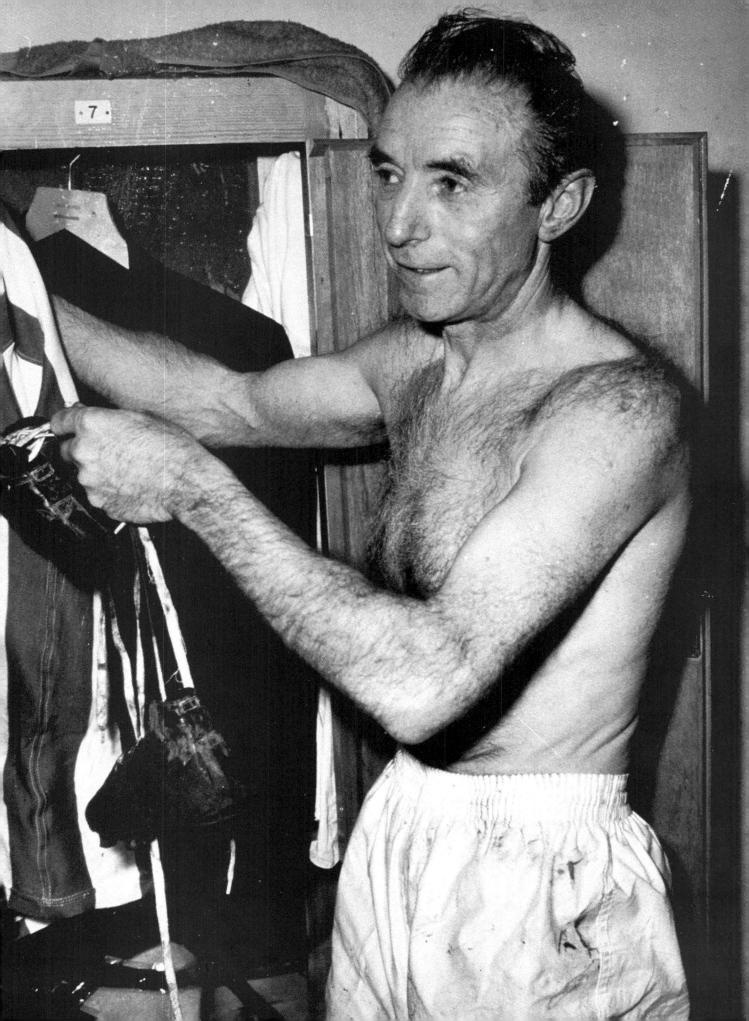

The transition from Hotspur-style boots to the low-cut lightweight boot was plain to see in CWS models.

leather in the toe-cap area gave them a greater feel of the ball, and enabled them to bend it with incredible precision, particularly at dead-ball situations such as free-kicks and corners.

Matthews was not content to simply marvel at the miracles the Brazilians were performing with their feet. He decided to do something about it, acquired a pair of the Brazilian boots and took them back home to study.

Once in England, Sir Stanley approached Mr J Grainge, works manager of the CWS (Co-operative Whoesale Society - the 'Co-op') footwear factory in Heckmondwike, and asked if he could produce a pair similar to the ones he had brought back from

Brazil. Mr Grainge was up to the challenge, and the first pair he made, the 45-45, weighed 1lb 9oz, unheard of in those days. He managed to reduce the weight even further for the next pair, the H90, which weighed in at 1lb 6oz.

Mr Grainge excelled himself for the 1956 England v Germany International, when he produced a pair for Sir Stanley which had neither toe puff or heel stiffener. These lightweight boots would normally last him 5 or 6 matches, and he always wore a brand new pair for Internationals and Cup-ties. Unlike the heavier models, they did not have to be broken in, and Mr Grainge would often get a phone call from Sir Stanley, asking that he send a pair to a particular hotel, from where the footballing legend would go straight to the opposition's ground and wear the boots straight from the box.

The boots themselves were made of light glace kid leather, without eyelets, and Mr Grainge would personally supervise all the components, weighing each part as it was produced. The boots had no studs, and were described in the sales blurb as "the lightest in the world, and the best in the world." On them were based the H91 model for adults, and the H77 and H78 models for boys. More than half a million pairs were sold between 1950 and 1958.

Further developments resulted in the weight

of the boots being reduced to 10oz, the flatter toe puff giving ample protection whilst adding little to the weight. Sir Stanley described them as being ". . . so soft, without toe caps, you could fold them up and put them in your pocket. Oh, they were beautiful! I used to sit and look at them, and feel the pleasure that they gave me."

Sir Stanley continued to have his boots made by CWS for many years, the company marketing a wide range of styles, all with his endorsement. A promotional film, *Magic Feet* was made in 1955, showing how the lightweight boots enhanced his footwork for both Blackpool and England. Aimed at adults and schoolboys, the 9-minute CWS →

Borrowed Boots

Sir Stanley Matthews hung up his boots in 1965, at the ripe old age of 50. Less widely known is the fact that the famous footwear claimed one final League goal later that year. It was for Port Vale, the club Matthews followed as a youth and was then managing. A Scottish teenager called Roddy Georgeson borrowed the maestro's pair and scored a goal in the game against Rochdale.

Football boots embraced 'continental' style long before the game itself in England did.

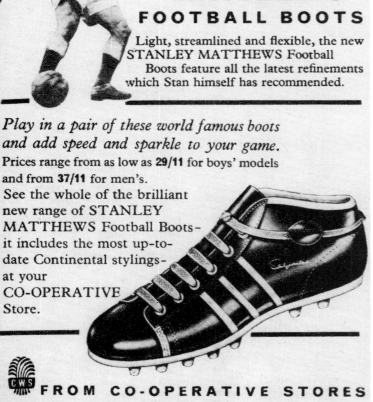

Whereas boots were once sold on their rigidity, flexibility became the name of the game.

So good he could 'have his cake and eat it' . . . in the shape of a pair of boots, of course!

film featured highlights of Matthews in the 1953 FA Cup final helping Blackpool to their famous 4-3 win over Bolton Wanderers. The player himself would often make promotional appearances at CWS shops throughout the country, signing autographs on the Saturday morning before joining the team in the afternoon for their game in that town. The days of actively using a footballing star to sell boots had truly arrived.

Meanwhile, the boffins at Heckmondwike were indefatigable in their quest for the ultimate football boot. Whilst most teams in the English and Scottish leagues at the time were soldiering on with the old fashioned knock-in studs, CWS were busily pioneering a variety of studs suitable for all kinds of pitches; screw-on aluminium, moulded rubber, leather, nylon or polystyrene. Sir Stanley himself used to take half a dozen pairs of boots with him to matches, all with different types of studs. After examining the pitch, he would decide which to wear – long when the ground was heavy or the grass was long, and shorter for a hard, bare ground.

In 1961, Sir Stanley, by then a Stoke player, came to the rescue of his team-mates before a 2nd Division league game against Bury. Stoke had decided to play in rubber-studded boots because of the hard pitch, but found they were 8 pairs short. Matthews, injured at the time and unable to play, phoned up Mr Grainge at Heckmondwide and asked if 8 pairs of his new rubber-studded moulded boots could be sent to Bury. The boots arrived in time for the players to take the field. They won the game 2-0.

This particular boot, the H46, was much lauded by the Stoke players, and players from other English sides, for its comfort and gripping power. It had 17 direct-moulded studs as opposed to the usual 12, and featured reduced toe spring and arching under the instep to allow the foot to be naturally poised. The toes were closer to the flatter toe cap, allowing the player to 'feel' the ball far better than before. This flatter toe cap, which was slightly extended, gave improved instep

control of the ball in passing, and greater accuracy in shooting. The boot was cut low round the ankle and padded with foam rubber bound with soft white leather. The tongue was padded as well, and a foam sock insert served to absorb shock. The cost of these boots in 1962 was 62s 6d a pair.

The team at Heckmondwike, moreover, were not averse to using sales gimmicks to further promote their products. In 1962 the H49 was introduced. similar in style to the H46, with 17 studs, low cut ankle and flatter toe cap. These beauties stood out from the crowd because they were blue in colour, with a white rubber sole, white facings and white instep straps. For the daring players who wanted to go one better, the boots were supplied with a choice of lace colour; white, red or yellow.

At that time, CWS boots from Heckmondwike were being worn by 6 English Football League clubs and one Scottish Division One team. One cannot help but think that had the originality of thought which went into the design of the boots been matched by a tad more originality in the naming of them, then this figure might have been even more impressive.

Nevertheless, the importance of Sir Stanley Matthew's involvement with CWS in the overall picture of the development of football boots this century cannot be overestimated. As he admitted himself, when he started out on his long career as a professional footballer at the age of 16, he was not particularly fussy about the type of boots he wore. He was undoubtedly not alone in this, but his vast experience in wearing boots in all kinds of weather, and in practically every country in the world where football is played, led him to think long and hard about how the tools of his trade should be styled and shaped. His thoughts on the weight footballers were carrying on their feet, coupled with his desire to "keep up with the youngsters who come along season after season" went a long way towards ensuring that boots would never be the same again.

SHORT PASS A nine-minute film called *Magic Feet*, made in 1955, featured highlights of Stanley Matthews in the 1953 FA Cup Final. It was used to promote the lightweight boots developed by CWS.

The second half

FOOTBALL BOOTS WOULD NEVER BE THE SAME AGAIN. Stanley Matthews set the ball rolling under his lightweight, flexi-soled boot, leaving leaden-footed full backs sprawling in his wake. The 1950s kicked off with new stars, new boots and new horizons. The 50s can truly be described as the decade that saw the most dramatic change in the style and development of football boots. In fact, on these shores at least, it was the decade that saw the boot turn into a shoe.

The lighter weight shoe had been in general use abroad for many years. In fact, Argentinian players were wearing low-cut shoes as far back as the 1920s. Back in Britain, in the 1950s, the cumbersome caterpillars were only just beginning to turn into butterflies.

By 1951, the International Board, following up results of questionnaires by the FA relating to foot care, footwear and the multitude of studs that were being made available, gave permission for screw-in studs of leather or rubber to be worn. Although screw-ins had been available for a couple of years, as included in the low-cut Puma models from 1950, this however first came to wide public awareness in 1954 at the World Cup in Switzerland. The West German soccer team wore Adidas boots with studs that screwed in and could be changed according to ground conditions. World Cups, →

SHORT PASS Jimmy Hill remembers buying boots two sizes too small and sitting with them on in the bath to help break them in.

47

a focus for soccer enthusiasts everywhere, allowed superb advertising opportunities.

Now players would have to consider an accessory other than a tin of dubbin or a pair of spare laces; a stud spanner of a kind that is still widely used today.

In 1955 the International board framed a new law. Studs could now be made of leather, soft rubber, aluminium, plastic or similar material. Continental designs influenced a change in style in British made boots.

The continental game was gradually influencing our own, and the boot was on its way to becoming more streamlined. Manfield, who still

manufactured the big, heavy boots which were looking increasingly prehistoric, were keen to be seen as a market leader, and placed themselves at the forefront of a fast developing market. They were making the Manfield Continental Mark 2 soccer boot. The leather was fairly thick and it still had a very solid toe-cap, but it had much lower sides and a moulded sole containing 20 studs set at varying heights.

Possibly due to the fact that concern was being voiced over injuries to the ankle or uncertainties as to whether this new idea was a fad or not, most manufacturers were not as bold as Manfield and seemed hesitant to go from ankle coverage to

Rubber studs with their own mounting plate (through which nails were driven into the sole) .

The 1954 World Cup finals in Switzerland provided marketing opportunities for the big manufacturers.

This picture of a low-cut Puma model from the 1950s shows how much progress was being made with 'continental' styling.

FREE KICK

In the aftermath of the Munich air disaster, Jack Crompton, who had just left his coaching job at Luton to help out at Old Trafford, was given the unenviable task of overseeing the unpacking of the skip containing the playing kit from the Red Star game.

Nobby Stiles was still on the ground staff, and he remembers opening the skip retrieved from the scene of the crash. "My job was to clean the boots. It was a heavy, shitty pitch and the boots were full of caked mud. When I finished, I asked Jack if I could keep Tommy Taylor's boots as a memento. He said "OK" I kept them for years, then I gave them to the club museum."

 SHORT PASS Garrincha, the wing wizard in Brazil's 1958 World Cup winning team, sometimes wore his left boot on his right foot and his right boot on his left. He said he could make the ball do more tricks that way!

ankle exposure in one bold cut of the pattern.

The boots worn and marketed by the leading players of the day do not clearly indicate any major change, but on closer examination we see that the leg portion of the upper has been reduced. Progress? Headlam & Sims Ltd. introduced their Sleekline and Streamline boots and the sales literature demonstrated that no only were they 'with it', they were gradually becoming 'without it', (the upper leg portions, that is). Some models show extra long tongues, flat-folded down, (nearly forty years before trendy teenagers hit the streets with rampant tongues hanging out of designer 'training' shoes) and why not? Players had been

doing this since the 1920s. As well as folding the tongues, players had been turning down the top rim of the ankle portion once the leather had softened. Obviously, if you are going to run around chasing leather in a pair of boots it is more comfortable to play with more freedom and less restriction to the ankle joint. In effect, the players' actions were dictating to the manufacturers the way ahead; they'd be fools to ignore the people who really mattered.

At this time the weight of the boot was lessened by another factor; the type of sole. Football boots, which had up until recently been made completely of leather, weighed around $\longrightarrow$

Oddballs

Bootlessness in the early part of the second half of the century seemed to be very much in vogue, with poorer Third World countries in particular showing a penchant for the bare-footed look. Sir Stanley Matthews recalls an international in Kenya in 1957 when he faced a bootless African known as "the fastest thing on two legs." Aided by his lightweight CWS boots, he found he could beat the Kenyan for speed over the first 12 yards - all he needed to gain the upper hand - but he was nevertheless amazed at how the opponents thought nothing of punting the ball from one end of the field to the other, wearing only elastic bandages around their ankles for support.

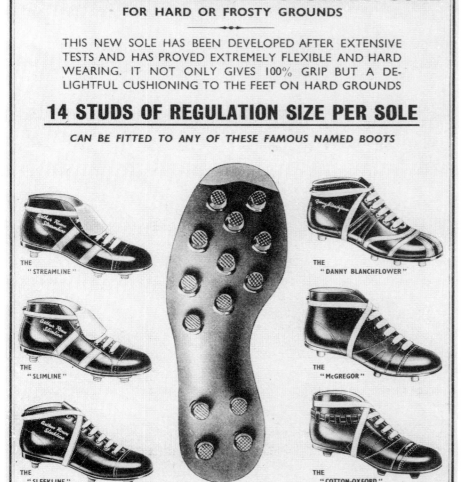

Spot the difference. Or were laces, stripes and tongues sufficiently different enough?

500g (1.1lb) when dry but almost doubled in weight when wet. Ninety minutes of football is tiring enough, and heavy-legs took on a new meaning when the feet got literally heavier and heavier as the game went on.

Manufacturers realised that even the best players were only in contact with the ball for short periods of the game, and actually spent most of their time running off the ball, and therefore they concentrated research on making their boots as light as possible. New man-made materials, such as plastic and nylon, developed during World War 2, were an integral part of that research and helped revolutionise the footwear industry.

The multi-studded sole, first produced by Adidas in 1949 and made of micro-cellular resin rubber, was becoming popular with pros and amateurs alike. As well as being more comfortable on hard and frosty grounds, they exerted less pressure on the sole of the foot than nailed-in

leather studs. Also, a new 'anti-mud' compound provided advantages over the traditional Dubbin. It let the vapour through the surface it was applied to but kept moisture out, whilst the dubbin stopped the leather from breathing. Neither did the sole collect as much mud as its leather counterparts.

The advent of television, which you could argue changed our lives for better or for worse, encouraged a distinguishing design feature in football boots. The logo. Although previously featured in some makes, it became vitally important as an indicator of brand distinction. Adi Dassler was reputedly the first shoe manufacturer to devise such a treatment. The three stripes, which are simple but extremely effective, were initially designed for functionality in the shoes, offering the feet additional support and stability during use. People recognising them instantly knew the brand and a logo was born. →

The first Puma factory, in Germany. Rudi Dassler is far right.

SHORT PASS Whilst manager at Aberdeen, Alex Ferguson forced Joe Miller to wear a pair of 1950 Puma boots for two weeks at training after he played a particularly bad game.

Broken in

Another logo which is instantly recognisable and which dates back to the late 1950s is the sweeping formstripe of Puma, one of the first and most eye-catching 'go-faster' stripe motifs and universally recognised in the footballing world. Even if you couldn't play with great style, you could look the business by wearing an instant classic.

Puma created the 'King' of football boots. Legends more often than not begin life in humble surroundings and the 'Puma King' emerged from a factory in Skutec, a small town deep in the Czech Republic. Players like Pele and Eusebio didn't wear boots because a whopping great cheque was waved under their agent's nose over a boozy lunch. They wore the Puma King because it was all that they wanted in a football boot.

Making football boots is a complex process and one where a surprising amount of hand-finishing still takes place. Ever heard of Pittards leather? Did you know that Kangaroo leather was widely used in football boots because of its durability? Was Chris Waddle wearing Kangaroo leather boots when he took that penalty in the 1990 World Cup?

For the Puma King, the manufacturing process starts with the various components of the Pittards upper and the synthetic lining being cut. This includes the heel, toe-piece and tongue. A pressing machine with sharp-edged pattern cutter attachments is used for this process, with an emphasis on ensuring a minimum of material wastage. The various components are then transferred to the 'closing' area of the factory floor. Here approximately twenty team-mates display better close control skills than Peter Beardsley on a good day, as they carry out the precision tasks of

Pittards WR100 Soccer Plus

LOW WATER UPTAKE

Pittards WR100 absorbs very little water. This demanding test, which mimics water surrounding the boot on a wet pitch for the duration of a game shows that an ordinary Kangaroo leather upper of 200g will almost double in weight over that period.

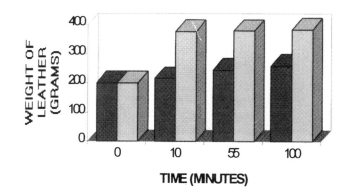

Comparison of Pittards WR100 Soccer Plus with Kangaroo Static Water Uptake test based on 200g uppers

It's simple; if you wear kangaroo leather you'll get soggy and wet.

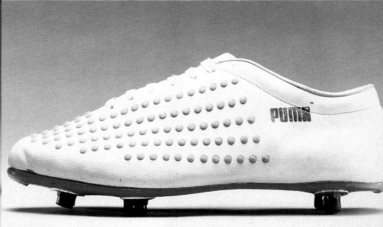

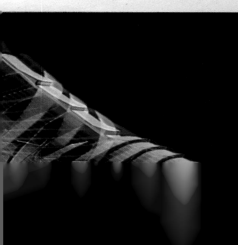

● Pele's right boot from the 1970 World Cup Final in which Brazil beat Italy 4 – 1.

● A Puma 'Red Dragon' from the early 1950s.

● The Puma 'Atom', made from 1948-1954 and a very early Dassler soccer shoe design.

● The future present – an incredible

● A Puma boot from the 1958 World Cup Final, signed by the Brazilian team.

● One of the first low-cut boots with screw-in studs, from 1950.

● It is hard to believe that this futuristic-looking boot was made by Puma in 1958 – it has ceramic 'pimples' stretching from the toe across the instep and sides of the boot.

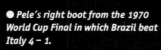

marking, stitching, bonding and lining. The boot starts to take on a recognisable shape when the upper components are glued and double-stitched together. Medial/lateral support overlays and a heel counter are added to provide protection with an ankle collar and a fold-down tongue then included for additional support.

With the body now whole, but searching for its sole, the second half of the process begins. The upper vamps are fitted around their corresponding size of wooden last and a gripping device tightly pleats, tucks and shapes the leather around an insole with the power of a Norman Hunter tackle. The upper is glued and tacked to the insole and then prepared for the bonding on of the dual-density outsole with a Duoflex zone on the Pro model. A direct moulding machine swiftly injects a polyurethane bi-density outsole onto the King Top

model. Stud threads, then studs, are inserted in the Pro and both models are then 'crowned' by the gold stamping of KING.

The Puma Formstripe is only one of a number of instantly recognisable logos which grace the feet of professionals and amateurs alike. Football is more than a game – an old cliche but perfectly true. It is art, passion, life, entertainment and a commercial opportunity. Boot manufacturers knew that by spending thousands getting players to wear their product, they could make millions as viewers developed a desire to obtain the boots worn by their heroes.

Two of the market leaders in the football boot world have clashed studs since 1948. The two heavyweights in question are Adidas and Puma or, just to make it fair, Puma and Adidas. This great rivalry emerged from a rift between two →

In March 1995, the football boot at last got the recognition and standing that it so long deserved. Yes, a magazine was at last named 'Boot' and it wasn't a pornographic one! Boot, a magazine for collectors of football programmes and memorabilia 'kicked off' and to boot each issue has, wait for it, an illustration of a boot on the cover. Pass our anoraks, please!

The earliest form of one of the best known logos in football.

gifted brothers; Adi and Rudi. They had made and sold sports shoes combining skill and superb craftsmanship under the name Dassler Brothers since 1924. In 1948 their increasingly profitable partnership ended sourly. After bitter family feuding, (local rumour has it that it was over either politics or a woman), Adi formed a company which became Adidas and operating in the same small German town of Herzogenaurach, Rudi formed Puma. Fierce competition between these two sporting giants has been a stimulus to the development of new ideas in shoe design.

An advert from 1959 clearly shows the Puma stripe, as well as boasting that the World Cup finalists of the previous year, Brazil and Sweden, were both loud in praise of the product. It is clearly lower down the ankle than most British made boots of even a couple of years before, and a feature that we all now take for granted is mentioned; interchangeable studs.

Billy Wright, who had his own name on boots in 1955 and was now playing on Puma's side, was typical of someone who was a good sportsman and in the public eye. Yes, the best players were reaping the benefits of their stardom.

Artex were plugging football boots, as used by the world famous Hungarian national team, in British sports magazines in the mid 50s. They →

If you can't beat them, join them seems to be the message from Artex.

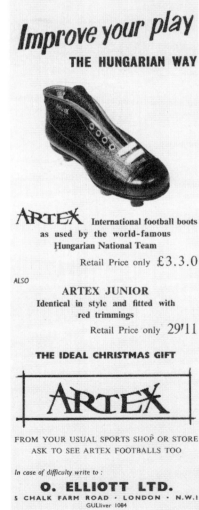

A very early football boot design by Rudi Dassler, who went on to form Puma.

Das ◯ des Columbus

ist die ges.gesch.
Riemenführung
beim

PUMA-fußballstiefel

Artikel 64.

Broken in

John Hollins was a trainee when Terry Venables was in the Chelsea first team. "I used to clean the boots every day," recalls Hollins. "After Jimmy Greaves had left for AC Milan, I came across a pair of boots on Greavsie's old peg. Terry told me Greavsie had left them for me, that I was the player to fill his boots. They were too small for me but I spent three weeks running around in them thinking I was destined to be the best before I discovered they weren't really his at all.

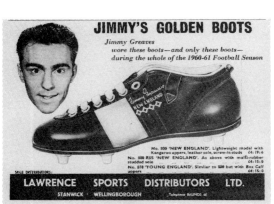

Jimmy's boots – where are they now?.

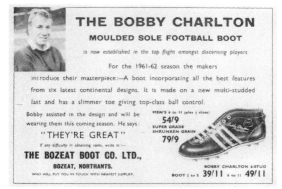

"They're great" roared Bobby (with real hair).

were no doubt hoping that the memory of the 6-3 drubbing of England was still fresh in the memories of sports readers. Youngsters aspiring to play for England were invited to *Improve your play the Hungarian Way*.

This adoption of star players and teams became increasingly important as the number of potential customers had been growing steadily since the beginning of the 20th century. Television stars wearing branded boots were a direct link, connecting living room minds to public park feet. Pages in sports magazines were filled with advertisements picturing smiling players (presumably because they were making a few bob) who had

obviously searched their imaginations to find phrases to describe how good the only boots they would wear were. Bobby Charlton, who was perhaps smiling because he still had hair, demonstrated his potential, as a rival for Tony the Frosties Tiger perhaps.

Many manufacturers were now describing their boots as being continental in style. The toes, which had previously come in three choices – hard, bloody hard or extra hard – were now softer, for 'greater ball control' and in many cases slimmer.

Comfort is also highlighted with padded tongues, toplines and insoles. Some manufac-

A youthful Jimmy Greaves shows off his ball control.

turers, however, were content with their boots being described as 'continental', and specified that their boots were 'Italian' style – sleek and stylish, perhaps. This vague marketing went one step further by stressing that the boot was continental in style but was made by British craftsmen. This was a clear message to potential customers that they would be getting the best of both worlds.

The advert from 1961 for Simlam, a continental sounding contraction of Headlam and Sim, shows a variety in the height of the ankle portion, suggesting that there was still a market for both tastes but more likely signifying that they were slipping behind their continental competitors.

Calling a boot the 'Toledo', even though it looked like every other boot in the range (including the 'Red Devil', doesn't make it any more attractive.

What people wanted was to feel like a famous player and in the days when you were likely to be told to 'push off' if you turned up at a club and asked to buy a team shirt there was no other way of getting close apart from buying your hero's boots.

Tottenham Hotspur, the 1961 cup-winners, appeared in an advertisement wearing Adidas boots – what better incentive for a young Spurs fan to emulate his idols. A closer reading reveals that the team merely trains in Adidas boots, perhaps saving their best boots for Cup Finals. →

If you couldn't play like an Italian you could at least look like one.

So whose boots did they actually wear for the final?

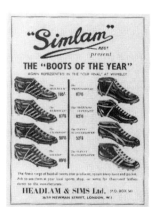

Simlan; still searching for that elusive distinguishing feature.

SHORT PASS Raquel Welch kicked off a Chelsea match in the 1960s wearing high heels. The crowd noises this spectacle produced were later used as part of the sound track to *A Million Years BC*.

57

The use of colour in magazine advertisements opened new doors for manufactures to promote their products. The sixties was a technicolour decade and football didn't escape the treatment. Kaftans, beads, long hair, mini skirts and George Best's Stylo Matchmakers. Colour was becoming increasingly important in the look and style of soccer shoes; lace, trim, sole and stud could all be other than black. With the sixties now beginning to swing, looking distinctive could now be achieved on the park as well as in the High Street. If you couldn't be colourful you could at least be comfortable. For a mere £6-19 shillings and sixpence you too could be as comfortable as Pele. In 1966, as well as being the world's best player, he was also the most comfortable. The reason? He got Barratts of Northampton to make his boots. According to an advertisement in *Soccer Star* of June 1966, Barratts presumably did not approach Pele to negotiate a fee to endorse their product, but instead Pele got them to make his boots!

A conversation between Pele and a representative from Barratts during his stay in England for the 1966 World Cup probably went like this;

Pele: I'm Pele and I wondered if you would be so kind as to make me a pair of football boots? I'd like really comfortable ones because as well as being the best player in the world, I also aim to be the most comfortable. Perhaps you could make them with a 3-piece tongue for added flexibility and comfort?

Rep: You're Pele, the world's greatest football player, and you want us to make your boots?

Pele: Yes, and with a luxurious foam-padded top line and sole.

Rep: That will be comfortable. Are there any other requirements, Pele?

Pele: Yes, a specially designed heel support for extra strength.

Rep: Consider it done, Pele. One last thing – do you mind if we use your profile as 'the world's greatest footballer' as a marketing tool to boost sales figures of similarly comfortable boots which aim to retail at £16-9s-6d and sell to millions of footballers who absolutely adore you?

Pele: No problem. After all, you're doing me a favour by making me the most comfortable boots in the world, aren't you? But perhaps you ⟶

The Barratts Managing Director, Paul Ziff, talks boots with the master.

could do one last thing for me? Could you possibly put my name on the side of my new, comfortable boots, just in case I lose them?

So Pele, with every boot manufacturer in the world clamouring for his endorsement of their product, 'got' Barratts to make his boots. The truth was that Paul Ziff, managing director of Barratts at the time, orchestrated a move which was surely the ultimate commercial coup of the 1966 World Cup (World Cup Willie excepted, of course).

Presumably had Pele scored a hat-trick in the final against England then Barratts might have expected to sell a few pairs of boots but the final-

ists that year, just in case anyone has forgotten, were England and West Germany. That fateful day, Hurst was wearing boots manufactured in West Germany by Adidas.

With the German giants of Puma and Adidas making boots and exporting them to most of the soccer-playing countries on the planet, their stylish French neighbours also attempted to get in on the action in 1967. Like Barratt, they played the 'comfort' card, but not the Pele one. French manufacturers 'Ours' loudly proclaimed their Chaussures Francaises Fantastiques (ahem, fantastic French shoes), a professional model

A French slip-on – style without practicality.

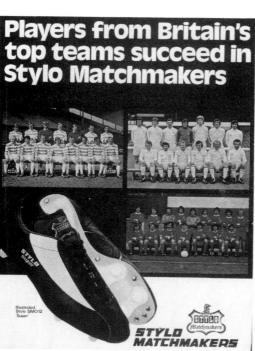

Everyone who wore Matchmakers succeeded to some extent.

"Put yourself in my shoes" said George. Years on many were glad they hadn't.

which included a feature, or lack of feature, not seen since the 1870s; boots without laces! Yes, a slipper with studs. They were without the high elasticated sides this time, but they did have an elasticated bridge below a tongue which doubled as a smoother striking area. Although the possible problem of a laced area causing a ball to shoot off in an unwanted direction was now solved, another problem arose. Boots which were easy to slip on could also slip off without laces to stop them. Comfortable they may have been around the home but for some reason they never really caught on. Innovation was far from dead however and it's

back to those Stylo Matchmakers again.

Stylo Matchmakers produced boots with a smooth striking area and laces at the side and carrying the name of George Best. With 'Gorgeous George', glamour personified, endorsing the product, it didn't really matter that they looked like a cross between a Chelsea boot and a Druid sandal. He epitomised style so the boots epitomised style. In one scribble of George's signature, Stylo had arrived. Kids everywhere, with pretensions not only to be a footballer, but one that oozed hip, would have done anything to step into Stylos. →

FREE KICK

When Trevor Francis was a youngster, his father used to take him out at night to practice with a ball. He would insist that Trevor work with only one foot for an entire session, then the next time he would use only the other foot.

Trevor stood by this policy, and it was advice which he passed on to any youngster who was not a natural two-footer. In the old days, he had heard, it was not unusual to see a player, even a recognised first team regular, practising with a boot on one foot and the thinnest of slippers on the other, to encourage the use of the weaker foot.

At a time when you could buy shoes with animal tracks on the sole, (and a compass in the heel) why not one with a George Best imprint.

SHORT PASS George Best received £20,000 up front and a 5% royalty on every pair of Matchmakers sold, for endorsing and wearing Stylo boots.

61

Ken Stanley, George's manager at the time, captured a great deal for the superstar – £20,000 up front and 5% of every pair of boots sold. Mr Stanley said, "If George had endorsed stair-rods they'd sell millions of them; his name meant so much." It seemed George couldn't fail, at least not while he was a positive role model. Sadly, history shows us that the positive turned to negative, and various sponsorship deals, including that with Stylo, disappeared.

Another boot marketed at impressionable kids (and perhaps parents of these kids who hoped their offspring would develop into the next George Best) were Power Points. Officially recommended by the English Schools FA, Powerpoints came with a free booklet crammed full of vital information. The secret of how to play winning football was at last being revealed . . . with stickers? Simple, eh? Stickers stuck onto strategic points of the boot: on the outer, on the inner, on the heel. These 'removable numbered target areas', as they were lovingly called, would do wonders for our game according to the adverts. Everyone at school seemed to have a pair. Wonder what happened to Powerpoints? And our game, come to think of it.

If Power Points were racy more was to come with the advent of white boots. There was always one or two lads in the school team who wore white

Playing by numbers with the mighty Power Points.

White boots by Patrick is a bit like "hair by Tracey".

boots and generally they were like the boots themselves – pretentious and unnecessary.

Seeing the human fireball himself explode in his white boots was as much a sight of the seventies as Alan Hinton streaking down the wing for Derby before gracefully gliding over a cross for Kevin Hector to head over the bar.

Now, you could be forgiven for thinking that that nice Martin Peters was a sensible sort of chap and not one to lend his name to anything remotely questionable. Remember the 'accuracymaster' – a strip of white something (also endorsed by Ferenc Puskas I might add) which covered the laces completely and looked like a shin pad had been

glued to the front of the boot? No? I don't either. No wonder there was a money **back** guarantee. Who knows why they didn't catch on. Perhaps it was because they looked too different, perhaps the claims seemed too good to be true, or perhaps it was the danger that the popular saying, "You couldn't lace his boots" would be lost to our game forever.

Manufacturers Hummel, Patrick and Adidas, amongst others, catered for the players who wanted to stand our from the crowd and be noticed. Team photographs from the early 70s show individuals brave, or stupid, or greedy enough to wear them. White boots, →

There was nothing that wearers of white boots couldn't do.

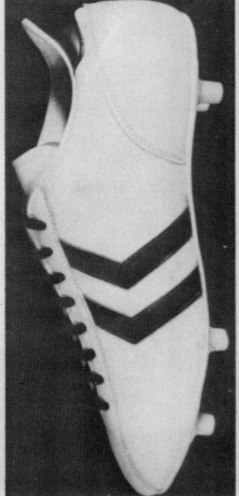

Explode into fits of laughter more like.

SHORT PASS Chris Waddle grew up with Power Point boots and used the numbered stickers on the toe, heel, outside and inside of the boot to improve his passing and shooting skills.

Broken in

Craig Brown recalls that the 1961 Dundee FC team were absolutely meticulous about looking after their boots. Not only did they polish the leather uppers; they also polished the soles, the idea being that the mud would not stick to the leather and possibly slow the players down, or otherwise interfere with their performance. Laces were white, and washed after every game. Studs were unscrewed after every game, and screwed back in on the Friday. No doubt they also gave the terracing a quick once-over with a duster on a Saturday morning!

predictably, attracted extra attention to those players who wore them. Excellent news if the player was having a good game, but bad news if not. Terrace-taunters generally don't require invitations before voicing verbal vitriol, and any players not doing the business with the leather sphere and wearing boots that screamed out, "I wanna be different – even though I look like a prat", were setting themselves up as easy targets. Other difficulties included opposition players being cautioned for having hacked away at your ankle, using the excuse of, "I thought it was the ball, ref. All I saw was a white blur." Keeping white boots 'white' also presented players with problems.

Once the outer skin of leather got scuffed, the brown below became obvious. Muddy winter conditions also made them look less than elegant.

Cheetah Sports also produced a boot with a wedge-shaped striking pad, this time with laces at either side. Their attempt at changing our perception of 'positional correctness' only succeeded in tingling the toes of a few. It seemed Joe Public, who could be seen wearing two-tone loons and a skinny rib tank top in the local High Street, was as traditional as bangers and mash when it came to strutting his studs. Boots with a difference has as much chance of succeeding as Jimmy Hill had of winning the title of 'small chin of the year'.

West Germany – Adidas wearers to a man.

Holdall: in two sizes.

"If you want to make the most of your ability, get the right kit," says Peter Shilton.

Skill and determination will take you a long way. But to exploit your ability to the full, you can't make do with second-best kit.

That's why professionals like Peter Shilton – and serious amateurs too – choose Cheetah Sports

You'll find everything a footballer needs under the Cheetah Sports colours: football boots, training shoes, track suits, holdalls – the lot. All designed by men who know what footballers want. (Ask Peter Shilton, he helped us to develop the Cheetah Sports range)!

CHEETAH SPORTS

Designed for the game as it's played today!

Coloured training shoes – style 333

Side-face boot - style 433   Conventional face boot - style 200   Pro-trainer

See them all at your local sports store. Or contact the sole distributors: Grays of Cambridge Ltd, PO Box 7, Cambridge. GRAYS

Even goalkeepers got in on the endorsement act . . . but where did the money go?

SHORT PASS 12% of professional players over all divisions are contracted to wear a particular brand of boots; 31% in the Premier League; 16% in Division 1; 3% in Division 2. Professionals use on average three pairs of boots per season.

Although most companies boasted endorsements by top class professionals to promote their product, our old friends Simlan chose to use an unlikely triumvirate of talents; Mr Thompson, a polo-neck wearing school team coach; a sports dealer with no left ear cavity, and schoolboy Jimmy Dawson, who wore boots resembling Manfield Hotspurs – in the 1970s? These three appeared in a comic strip aimed at the school-kid market, Jimmy hits a form slump, asks polo-neck for advice, and is persuaded by alien ear to buy a pair of Simlams. Life after that becomes rosy. Jimmy has a jolly good game in jolly good boots and becomes a jolly good fellow.

As ever, the domestic game provided local interest and although Stylo Matchmakers were beginning to get a grip of home turf, signing up Liverpool, Leeds and Glasgow Celtic *en bloc*, they could not, however, halt the dominating progress of the two worldwide giants who were competing in a sales league of their own. Pele and Cruyff endorsed Puma, and the '74 and '78 West German World Cup teams wore Adidas.

Stylo, although clearly not in the same league as the market leaders, proved that through clever marketing they could threaten for a while at least. Controversy, however, may have had an adverse effect on their reputation. Fulham, FA Cup →

PUMA
SPORTSCHUHE 1967

PUMA IST AM BALL, DENN PUMA MACHT'S MIT QUALITÄT

Eusebio und seine geliebten PUMA-Schuhe

Contrary to popular belief, Eusebio always kissed his own boots.

finalists in 1975, had been contracted to wear Stylos during that year, but had secured a deal to wear Adidas for the final. With players eager to cash in on their success, this deal was one which would have made them more money. Stylo were understandably upset when this double-dealing came to their attention and threatened to sue Fulham, who, in turn, threatened to discredit the boots. Stylo tried to bring out a court injunction, forcing Fulham to stick to the original deal, but the judge decided to take a neutral stance; ordering the players to paint over the logos on their boots, so that they would be seen to be wearing neither Stylos or Adidas!

The market was increasing, and companies like Mitre, Power, Dunlop, and Gola amongst others battled away bravely to climb the sales ladder. Their tactical game plan remained the same; claim an innovation, have a flash logo, procure endorsement by a top player or coach and advertise in the football magazines. In the late 70s and early 80s, however, none could compete with the big two, who continued to dominate. Whereas Simlam recruited fictional characters in a black and white advert to sell their product, Adidas, promoting the Silverlines, adopted a similar approach but in full colour, taking up a whole page in soccer magazines. They were also endorsement by Trevor

FREE KICK

When the Golden Boot is awarded, a replica is made using the exact shoe size of the player involved. When it was awarded to Bill Shankly, who was a small man, he had no hesitation in stating that he wore a size 12!

Shanks on a blind date with number nine. Cilla's forgotten her boots again.

Simlan were still trying but not quite getting there.

SHORT PASS Asics make one of the most expensive pairs of boots available – the completely handmade TSS900 is around £200 per pair. The Reebok Supreme Cole sells for around £40, and a pair of Predator Cup will set you back almost £120.

Francis – a real person.

Of course, it had to happen. As boots took off in a big way in the 70s and 80s, it was only a matter of time before entrepreneurs the country over woke up to the financial possibilities 'football-related' merchandise offered. Companies suddenly took it upon themselves to jump on the bandwagon. Their aim? To milk every last penny from a gullible and highly receptive target consumer group.

Ruthlessly carving out vast chasms in the market which they, and they alone could fill with their product (how have I managed to survive for so long without a Foxley football boot key-ring?),

these companies shamelessly plied their trade. They seemed oblivious to the fact that the money spent on their goods was probably earned delivering morning newspapers in Arctic conditions and, more sinisterly, were blissfully unaware that what they had to offer more often than not reached uncharted depths of tastlessness.

But there's tack and there's tack, and if a prize had to be given for the ultimate in bad taste ideas, then a leading contender would have to be Steda Slippers for their innovative and highly desirable International Team Mates slippers. Note the subtle use of the word 'international', included to give the impression that the Dutch, the French →

Borrowed Boots

Some players turned borrowing boots into an art form. Mick Channon recalls playing alongside Brian O'Neill in the 70s. Brian apparently never owned a pair of football boots, and could often be found in the boot-room on match days rummaging around for anything he could find. On Fridays before away games the trainer George Horsfall would make sure the other first-team boots were packed before Brian could get his hands on a pair he fancied.

ADVERTISEMENT

Adidas had other ideas by writing Trevor Francis (complete with obligatory sheepskin) into comic history.

and the Germans would also be falling over themselves to buy a pair.

Two advertisements for these slippers demonstrate how important a player endorsement is in the selling of a product. You would surely not be attracted to this footwear for aesthetic appeal alone. The young boy in the picture looks as if he has got several newspapers stuffed up his pyjama top. The work of Saatchi and Saatchi it is not.

Now take a look at the later advert. Steda have managed to procure the endorsement of Martin Peters, a man well known and respected for his discerning taste in slippers, and the transformation is remarkable. The young armchair shopper,

faced now with an advert which brims with confidence and oozes class, simply wilts under the pressure and buys a pair. He has taken the first crucial step up the brand loyalty ladder, and were Steda to market a pair of slippers with foam studs and 'realistic' clumps of foam mud on the soles, then no doubt he would buy them as well.

You can imagine the conversation:

"If Martin Peters says that brushed bri-nylon with foam and Swansdown lining is where it's at, then that's good enough for me", the young Rambo says to his envious mates.

"But wait a minute, – you're trying to tell me that the elasticated laces need threading only

The pre – "why don't we ask Martin Peters to endorse our slippers" attempt . . .

A must for every classroom – sharpen your pencil and practice your "ball skill" at the same time.

SHORT PASS Nearly three-quarters of all professional players prefer a fold-over tongue on their football boots. 39% are opposed to colours other than black and white.

once – you're winding me up!"

"Straight up, lads, and while you're at it, take a butchers at the nylon stretch bar binding – are we talking a quality pair of loafers or what?"

"Yeah. You're right. There's no denying they're top-notch. Wow, just think. If I save really hard for the next six months I could have a pair!"

If the second advert could be faulted in any way, it would have to be for its omission of one crucial selling point; the fact that were the wearer to jump up and down hard enough on his bri-nylon sheets, enough electricity could be generated to power his Peter Osgood bedside table lamp for a whole evening.

Heliz International were another company who demonstrated such expertise in exploiting an opening when they saw one, although why the PFA would want to recommend a pencil-sharpener is anyone's guess. Nevertheless, three classy boot-related items of stationery are on offer here; the boot eraser set, the trainer pencil-case and the football boot pencil set. Young boys, their heads so full of football trivia that they were utterly useless at their lessons, could at least impress their friends as they pulled, from out of their football boot pencil case, their football boot eraser, invaluable as it was for rubbing out those mistakes made whilst day-dreaming about scoring a Cup-winning goal. →

FREE KICK

Some players, overcome with emotion, have been known to throw their boots into the crowd at the end of a particularly poignant 90 minutes. Tommy Burns of Celtic threw his boots to the fans after he had played his last game for the team Mo Johnstone did likewise after Watford had lost a Cup Final to Everton, singling out a small, tearful young fan as the honoured recipient. And Eric Cantona, playing his last game for Manchester United in the 1994/95 season (although he wasn't to know it at the time), threw his boots to a rather vociferous Crystal Palace fan. Unfortunately for both parties, Eric was still in them at the time.
Other fans have been luckier than have a pair of dirty boots flung in their face. Mrs J Hayes of Bolton was given John McGinlay's right boot at the end of the 1993/94 season after it had helped the Bolton player win the Golden Boot award. She has had it mounted on a piece of polished wood, and attached a small plaque telling the story of how she acquired it.

Martin Peters does his stuff.

Borrowed Boots

Before the 1986 World Cup in Mexico, the England squad stayed in Colorado and trained at the nearby US Air Force Academy.

Bryan Robson had forgotten to take his boots to training one day, and was wandering about looking for a pair of size 9s. Eventually he managed to borrow a pair, but throughout the session he complained about the pain in his feet. He ended the session limping quite badly, and moaning loudly that the boots could not possibly be size 9.

On closer inspection, Robson discovered that wads of tissue paper were still crumpled up in the toes.

And let's face it – any company that could persuade Justin Fashanu to endorse rubbers so early in his career must have had a lot going for it.

Moving slightly upmarket, AA Souvenirs tried to introduce a touch of class to the whole business with their pottery boot money-box, featuring lace and stud detail. A cunningly concealed slot on the base of the boot enabled the proud owner to obtain the coins which had been placed inside, and for the floating, hesitant buyer unsure of whether to part with their £2.29, the fact that they were fully glazed probably clinched it.

An interesting variation on a theme appeared in 1971 when Stylo Matchmakers launched their Striker shoes on an unsuspecting public. The whole concept is tantamount to marketing gone mad; a tough pair of shoes designed to be worn whilst playing football in the playground – the idea is mind-boggling in its ingenuity and sheer audacity. Stylo, with the backing of George Best, was the big boot company at the time, and one can only feel sympathy for the poor mums and dads who were forced to fork out week in week out to feed their sons' insatiable addiction to all things football-related. A marketing expert would no doubt have a stock phrase or buzz-word to explain the phenomenon – product creation on the back of an existing heavy brand awareness, or some

SHORT PASS Although Jurgen Klinsman signed a deal with Reebok in 1994, the German Federation insists he wears Adidas whilst playing for the national side.

twaddle like that, but to the man in the street it was just pure exploitation. There could be no doubt as to who had hacked you in the playground skirmish – the big imprint of Georgie Best on your calf was a sure sign that it was your mate with the Strikers who was responsible.

With one eye on a quick buck, these minnows of the football business world fed frantically off the boot industry, desperate to find the perfect product. It would appear that few, if any, were successful.

Boots are becoming increasingly lightweight and innovations, although not as earth-shattering as, say, the side-lacers, are still apparent. Soles are being made of a polyurethane in two or three different densities, studs are becoming widely available in a range of colours (and a range of lengths and type to suit varying conditions too), and strenuous efforts are being made to incorporate maximum flexibility, comfort and durability.

Companies talk to top players and coaches to get to know and understand their needs. Examples of this are Umbro, whose technical adviser is none other than the great Brazilian master Pele (a man who likes playing in comfortable boots); Mizuno, who work with David Platt; New Balance, who for many years were advised by Bryan Robson (who earned £25,000 a year for his trouble). →

These innovative boots featured in a *Daily Mirror* competition during the early 70s and were heralded as the greatest development since screw-in studs. Steve Perryman modelled these boots with swivelling stud foreplates and no doubt visualised himself pirouetting past static defenders.

Years later Perryman recalled the strange sensation when turning with the ankle, knee and hip joint remaining rooted to the spot and the ball of the foot alone determining movement. The fact that he never actually wore the boots in training, let alone in a game, but only in a twenty-minute photo shoot suggests he was far from impressed.

Needless to say, they didn't catch on.

A vintage Leeds side take their reading lesson outdoors – in Stylo Matchmakers, of course.

Broken in

When Eric Cantona was a junior and playing for Callois in the Provence Championship he had trouble getting a decent night's sleep. Horrible nightmares of monsters coming and eating his laces and leaving his boots in shreds made him wake up in the middle of the night to ensure the boots were at the same place at the foot of his bed and still in one piece.

A boot is like a Grand Prix racing car when it comes to finding places to place a logo. Why not put the logo on the heel, the sole, or the tongue? Why not make the tongue longer, say it's more comfortable and splash the brand name across it? Does it stand out enough? Perhaps not! Let's make it white, fold it down and emblazon it in a contrasting colour with the brand name. Now, even when a player has his back to the TV camera, writhing in agony on the ground, viewers will know which kind of boots that player wears.

One other aspect of recent times that parallels the increasing use of new technology and brand exposure has been the emergence of new compa-

nies and established sports goods companies diversifying into the football game. And why not? The boots market is worth tens of millions every year. This desire to get a bigger slice of the pie has led to a recent spate of bolder innovations, not just restricted to footwear that's worn on the field of play. Remember the suede finish on Adidas trainers in the seventies? You know, the sort worn by your parents when they went to play Badminton? A revamped range became hot street wear, and Puma have made available a stunning collection of leisure footwear based on Dassler classic designs – boots without studs designed to look good in the stands rather than in the mud.

The man with predatory instincts who put the hop, skip and swerve into football boots.

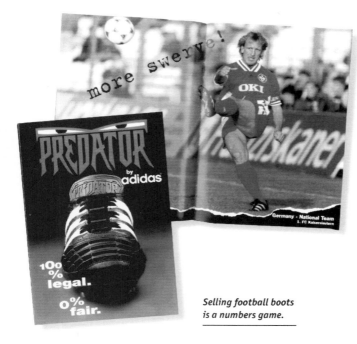

Selling football boots is a numbers game.

Is it a plane, is it a bird? No, it's the shark of football boots.

In 1994 the Predator emerged as the boot with more power, more swerve and threatening to improve every player on the team; except one – the goalkeeper. After departing Liverpool FC, the Australian footballer Craig Johnston seemed to disappear off the face of the earth, and people wondered what had become of him. A BBC TV documentary in April 1994 enlightened us. He's spent his time developing a new, 'revolutionary' type of soccer boot.

His inspiration was triggered off when a company approached him, wanting to do a Craig Johnston boot. Craig declined, because despite the fact that he described it as a beautiful shoe,

almost an elitist model, there were two aspects that he was unhappy with. It was not affordable to kids and it was manufactured from kangaroo leather. Fair dinkum Craig.

Johnston felt that conventional boots, being the opposite shape from the ball, did not offer enough contact area when striking it. Not only did he feel that they were the wrong shape, but he also believed that they were made from the wrong material. Leather, to his way of thinking, did not offer enough friction, especially when wet, to put bend or spin on the ball. Why not have the boot as an instrument specifically designed for getting the ball from A to B, to be a performance tool in →

Goalkeepers have hit back with special boots of their own.

terms of swerve, dip, bend and acceleration. Not an original thought surely. The result was the Predator, the latest in a long line of boots that have been designed to give more power or control.

His vision was that the sweet spot should be larger and flatter. A fellow Australian investor, who also felt that a material with greater friction would be more appropriate, approached Craig, the highest profile player he knew, to test out his own idea. Harold Hunter had covered a conventional boot in serrated plastic material that had been used to make conveyor belts. On testing the boot, Craig felt that this material definitely offered more grip, but it was too thick and therefore did not provide a proper feel for the ball.

Meanwhile, Craig's own research continued. He had noticed, whilst wind-surfing one day, that one-piece rubber-mould shoes made specifically for the sport by Okespor of France, offered good grip in the wet. At the Okespor factory on the outskirts of Paris, Craig was introduced to injection moulding, a process in which synthetic rubber

FREE KICK

WHO WEARS WHAT

Arsenal	Wright	*Nike*
Aston Villa	Bosnich	*Reebok*
Blackburn	Shearer	*Umbro*
Bolton	McGinlay	*Mizuno*
Chelsea	Gullit	*Lotto*
Coventry	Dublin	*Reebok*
Everton	Amokachi	*Puma*
Leeds	McAllister	*Asics*
Liverpool	Collymore	*Diadora*
Man City	Rösler	*Uhlsport*
Man Utd	Schmeichel	*Hummel*
M'boro	Barnby	*Quasar*
Newcastle	Gillespie	*Predator*
Notts Forest	Roy	*Lotto*
QPR	Hateley	*Nike*
Sheff Weds	Hurst	*Puma*
S'hampton	Le Tissier	*Quasar*
Spurs	Anderton	*Diadora*
West Ham	Moncur	*Mitre*
Wimbledon	Holdsworth	*Puma*

Boot Sponsorship

BOOT SPONSORSHIP IS PART AND parcel of the modern game. Fans seldom raise an eyebrow nowadays at the sums of money offered to players to wear particular boots, and boot companies are continually vying for an opportunity to promote their product.

In the early days of endorsements, a certain naivety and amateurishness tinged the company-player relationship, however, Craig Brown recalls that when leading players began to sign contracts with manufacturers to wear particular boots, they did not necessarily feel a great desire to wear the boots they endorsed. This led to ridiculous compromises, with the player often painting on imitation trademarks so that he could continue to wear his favourite brand whilst appearing to sponsor another.

Denis Law tells of a club manager striking up a deal for his whole team just before a cup-final. The players preferred the boots of a rival company, which differed only in that they had stripes running down the side. Their answer was to simply pull off the stripes, although anyone looking closely could see the marks where the stripes had been.

And revenge was sweet for the Scotland World Cup squad just before their 1974 game against Zaire. They had been promised money if they wore a particular brand. The money never arrived, and they spent the night before the match ripping off the manufacturer's logo.

Manufacturers themselves could be quite cavalier in their approach to winning player endorsement. When England were playing West Germany in a 1968 international in Hanover, representatives from both Adidas and Puma descended on the England camp, offering massive cash incentives for players to wear their boots. Several took the bait, and went into the match wearing the new boots. This, of course, was inadvisable as the boots had yet to be broken in, and Alf Ramsey did not hide his disgust that the players had jeopardised their teams' chances for money. England lost 1-0, a defeat that would have been particularly hard to swallow given the result of the World Cup final two years previously.

The modern relationship between player and company, coupled with more sophisticated advertising techniques, has

The legendary Roy Race – never a man to compromise on a deal.

and plastic melt when heated. It is forced under great pressure into a series of rotating moulds where it cools and solidifies in seconds into thermo-plastic rubber. Highly impressed by this process, Craig commissioned Okespor to make a prototype boot. A mould of one of Okespor's golf shoes was converted at a cost of £15,000.

Craig now had a second guinea pig boot to try out, which had a concave sweet spot. On testing, he felt that it held its shape in the air, thus providing more accuracy, but there wasn't enough

grip to provide spin. Craig, now obsessed with the idea of creating a new type of boot, was further inspired by thoughts of grooves cut into car tyres giving purchase when accelerating and braking. Spending many hours cutting various depths and patterns into rubber prototypes using engraving tools, he strived to find a satisfactory result, paring the rubber down and leaving protruding fins which gave five separate contact areas. This almost provided Craig with the satisfaction he craved, but despite the fact that there was an →

Oddballs

and Agents

resulted in a far more professional approach being adopted. Nike, for example, turned Eric Cantona's well-documented short-fuse temper to their advantage in 1994.

"I've been punished for striking a goal keeper . . . for spitting at a supporter . . . for throwing my shirt at a referee . . . and for calling my manager a bag of shit . . . Then I called the jury who punished me a bunch of idiots . . . I thought I might have trouble finding a sponsor."

No fear, Eric. The advert may have been accused of "bringing the game into disrepute", but the furore it caused ensured that the name Nike was firmly imprinted in the minds of potential customers. Eric, of course, took this concept quite literally in the infamous 'Crystal Palace supporter' incident, but he needn't have bothered.

JIM GABRIEL & ADIDAS BOOTS

I had just signed for Dundee in 1957, and although I was still playing for my junior team North End, I was required to train with Dundee two nights a week.

One night, before training

started, the Dundee manager Willie Thornton approached me carrying the strangest pair of boots I had ever seen. The boots were black in colour with three white stripes down the outside and inside of the instep. They also had some lettering on the side which spelled out the word Adidas. They looked much lighter than normal new boots, the toe-caps were softer, the uppers which protected the ankle lower, and there were no bars on the bottom to hammer the studs into. They were as far removed from my pair of Manfield Hotspurs as you could possibly get.

Mr Thornton told me that I could have them on condition that I wore them as soon as I had broken them in because they were a test pair of boots sent to the club by Adidas. As I was quite fascinated by these strange looking objects I immediately agreed to his conditions and set about breaking them in. This didn't take very long, less than a couple of weeks, because of their lightness and the softness

of the leather.

However, had I anticipated the reception I got from the North End supporters, players and club officials when I trotted onto the park sporting my new Adidas boots, I would probably have told Mr Thornton to give them to someone else. The Dundee football supporters were extremely conservative in their opinion on football boots, and the Adidas version did not meet the required standards as far as they were concerned.

However, once I'd played in them, I wasn't going to swap them for any other. They were as comfortable on my feet as made to measure boots, and my touch and timing, passing and control improved every time I wore them. Soon enough the spectators cat-calls turned to cheers and my team-mates' guffaws to questions like "Where can you buy them?" Adidas and I survived that early baptism of fire as we set off on our new professional football careers. →

75

improvement, the boots still lacked the stunning revelation that he desired.

The more explosive element that he was looking for was still unattainable. This requirement was met when Craig spotted a 'superball' in a toy shop – yes, the very same balls that we've all bounced the hell out of and lost. This explosive element, however, was not lost on Craig, He stuck parts of superballs to conventional boots and at last found the missing link.

His next move was to approach the innovation

department of Adidas in Nuremberg. Some of the people there were very sceptical, and one even walked out at the ridiculous idea of a rubber boot. However, they did agree to at least test the boot out. After carrying out their own hi-tech research, Adidas found that the boot provided 23% more swerve and 7% more velocity. Craig's dream boot, which he initially wanted to be affordable to kids and preferably not made from kangaroo leather, was to retail initially at £120 a pair, and included in its manufacture relatives of Skippy!

FREE KICK

In 1984, in North Carolina, schoolkid Mike Moylan had a hard time finding soccer shoes. To make it easier for himself and thousands of other soccer enthusiasts Mike, aided by his parents and brother Brendan, started a soccer shoe mail order company, Eurosport. This has grown from two telephones, eight employees, a cash register and a dream to a multi-million dollar company with over four hundred employees. As well as providing punters with hard to find soccer gear at reasonable prices, Eurosport's aim was to promote the growth and excitement of the world's greatest game. This aim to service the soccer community took a step forward in 1990 when the 'PASSBACK' programme was launched. Customers are asked to send in used (but still usable) soccer shoes in exchange for a $5 credit voucher. These returned shoes, as well as overstock and slightly defective ones, are distributed to needy players throughout the U.S.A. as well as Zimbabwe, Tanzania, Brazil, Gabon, Togo, South Africa, Bolivia and Japan.

Boot Sponsorship

AGENT PROVOCATEURS

Quite why the word 'agent' should strike such horror in the hearts of those in soccer's higher echelons is sometimes difficult to fathom. Whilst agents in other sports command respect, football agents are seen as guys in raincoats, out to line their grubby pockets and to hell with the players they purport to represent.

Bengal Harvey is widely regarded as the first football agent, although the bulk of his clients in the 1950s came from the world of cricket. His involvement with the likes of Denis Compton, Jim Laker and Fred Trueman tended to overshadow his football dabblings, partly because the authorities at the time did not make it easy for agents to operate in soccer. He was involved in Jimmy Greaves' move to Italy, but contented himself mainly with boot contracts and personal appearances, rather than transfers.

Since then, they have become as much part of the football scene as former players-turned-commentators. Evil villains, or vital cogs in the

financial machinery, there to protect often naive and vulnerable players from the cigar-smoking camel coat wearers who run football? Who can tell? Whatever the opinion, they exist, and can make young players very rich in no time at all. Transfers are obviously where both agent and player can make a mountain of money, but what about the role of the agent in boot sponsorship deals?

AN AGENT SPEAKS

Raymond Sparkes is one of the top agents in Scotland, representing the interests of as many as 55 football players at any one time. His agency, Pro Star Management, has attracted much media interest in the past, primarily due to the fact that Raymond currently handles the career of John Collins of Celtic, but he has many other talented players on his books, including Phil O'Donnell, Rob McKinnon and John Inglis.

Raymond's CV is impressive, having spent nigh on a decade with Hibernian FC first as marketing manager and latterly as commercial director, until he

decided to go it alone and form his own agency. It is the kind of experience which is invaluable in the cut-throat corridors of football's commercial labyrinth, and Raymond's current high status in Scotland is no doubt due largely to the network of contacts he was built up over the years.

When asked to outline his main role in his current position, he describes it as "career developer", and in the case of John Collins in particular you have a prime example of what exactly he means. An agent is out to get the best for his clients – that is what he is paid for after all – but it is not simply a case of negotiating transfer deals. We asked Raymond to elaborate on his role, especially in respect of football boot deals, and his answers give an insight into an often understated part of his operations.

What is your specific role in the boot sponsorship deal process?
My role principally is to unearth and bring together both parties, and once that has been achieved,

 SHORT PASS During the 1994 World Cup, Maradona played one game wearing Adidas boots and wore Puma boots in another – with the logos blacked out on both occasions. Seeking a boot deal perhaps?

The advent of the Predator saw a marketing campaign unrivalled by competitors. In sports shop windows the boots could be seen in cages behind mangled bars. Yes, the Predator was out to get you. You and your money! Clever adverts in soccer magazines and on television suggested that goalkeepers should fear them, but, costing as much as they did and with the promise of almost magical properties, it was perhaps the parents of football crazy kids everywhere who really feared the 'Beast'.

Pre-birthday and Christmas gift discussions – the modern-day battlefields of desire, determination, induced guilt and emotional blackmail were won only by the most tactically aware.

Emotional blackmailer: Mum, Dad, can I get a new pair of football boots for Christmas?
Parent: Are your old ones finished?
Emotional blackmailer: Yeah, they're falling apart and they don't fit anymore.
Parent: Oh, I suppose so.
Emotional blackmailer: Can I get Predators? ⟶

Borrowed Boots

In the first round of the 1994 UEFA Cup, Aberdeen played a Latvian team, Skonto Riga. The first leg in Latvia ended in a goalless draw. On his way to the second leg, the Skonto Riga striker, Alexei Semyonov, lost his luggage, and his boots ended up on a plane to Italy. Aberdeen loaned him a pair of boots, and he went on to score his side's goal in the 1-1 draw. Due to the away goals ruling, this was the goal which knocked Aberdeen out of the competition.

and Agents

to continue to negotiate and overlook the deal.

Do you as an agent actively seek out boot deals for your clients, or is it a case of the manufacturer coming to you?
It's sometimes a bit of both, but for the most part I actively look for deals for my players.

Boot manufacturers obviously target specific players to wear their product. What particular qualities do they look for before deciding to approach a player?
They're looking for a player who has talent, obviously, but it doesn't end there. A clean-cut image and reliability are also important, as well as an ability to endorse the product as a solid role model.

Can you give an idea of the range of money a sponsorship deal may be worth to players?
Players of one standard will wear boots for a simple bonus, whereas someone like Ryan Giggs can earn a six figure annual sum.

Once a player signs a deal, what is expected of him?
Once the deal is complete, the

player must wear and keep clean the boots. He will also be expected to actively endorse the product, through public appearances and other such PR work.

Do players test the boots before signing the deal, or do they wear them whatever?
Usually a player will wear the boots before putting pen to paper, but if the product is already established the chances are that he has worn them before and knows what they are like.

What might happen in the event of a breach of contract?
The deal may well be cancelled, or bonuses and retainer could be withheld.

When John Collins signed the deal to wear Predators, there was much press interest, in particular an article in the Daily Record. Who initiated that article - the press, the player or yourself?
In this instance I contacted the paper to inform them that the deal had been signed. The rest

was down to John.

ALAN SHEARER

In May 1995, Alan Shearer, the Blackburn Rovers and England striker, signed a new deal with Umbro worth almost £2.5 million.

The player, who started out with the sportswear giants by writing to the firm as a teenager and asking for a pair of boots, signed an 8 year deal believed at the time to be the most lucrative of its kind.

The deal meant that Shearer would receive a basic £250,000 a year for wearing their boots and equipment, plus incentives for international and club success, thus outstripping the £500,000 over 4 years that Ryan Giggs was reported to be receiving from Reebok.

Shearer heads for the bank.

Borrowed Boots

In the 1985 - 86 season, Gary Lineker was playing for Everton. Liverpool came from behind with a run of 11 wins and one draw to snatch the title from their Merseyside rivals. Everton paid dearly for losing 1-0 at Oxford, at the end of April 86. It's a game Lineker remembers for a miss that still haunts him.

"I had a chance, one-on-one. The keeper actually made a good save, but if that had gone in, we'd have won the league, I think. I've had a few embarrassing misses in my career – in fact, I've missed loads of chances – but if I had to nominate one, it would be the one at Oxford because it was so important. I lost my lucky boots that night. I'd scored something like 20 goals in 20 games, then forgot to put them in the skip. So I had to wear some borrowed boots. When I got my boots back, I scored 5 goals in the last 2 games. They were falling apart, but I had them repaired and took them to the finals of the 86 World Cup". (Where he finished top scorer with 6 goals.)

Parent: I though you wanted boots. Now you want a video. Make up your mind.

Emotional blackmailer: No, Predator football boots. You can swerve a ball more with them and they only cost £120.

At this point, parents scream, laugh deliriously or faint. This is followed by an account of their own Christmas when they were young, and how grateful they were to receive an apple, an orange and, if they were lucky, a spinning top.

Emotional blackmailer: Oh go on, Todd Johnstone's got a pair'; his parents must really love him.

Parent: Forget it. We'll go down to the sports shop and we'll choose boots together. There's no way you're getting Predators.

Emotional blackmailer: I'm phoning Esther Rantzen's Childline to ask if she'll adopt me.

For every new invention there's someone who says they were there first. Craig said "it doesn't ring a bell".

Another revolutionary boot to emerge in 1994 were Blades, invented by David Miers from, where else, Australia. Instead of conventional studs, the boots have rubber blades running diagonally along the sole. They are designed to allow a player to use more force on the outside foot during a turn. The blades are spread around the main pressure points to give greater support and reduce soreness from studs pressing into the heel and ball of the foot.

Although Craig Johnston and David Miers are the better-known players in the game of manufacturing football boots from Australia, there are thousands of others who play their part. In fact, they've played out of their skins for decades, and their supporters have only recently made any real impact in making it clear to team selectors that they'd rather not be involved at all.

Who are these selfless 'players' whose →

FREE KICK

Chris Waddle has fond memories of the Power Point boots, which had numbers on the toe, heel, inside and outside to help improve the wearer's passing and shooting skills. Chris said that the numbers used to come off every time he kicked the ball.

It is a little-known fact that these boots were largely responsible for his infamous penalty miss in the World Cup semi-final against West Germany. Apparently the German coach managed to sneak into the dressing room before the England team arrived and swopped the numbers round on Chris's treasured Power Points. Luckily this trickery did not lead to him attempting to back-heel the ball into the net from the spot, but nevertheless he was confused enough to miss the crucial spot kick.

Football's been played in boots with studs for over 80 years.

Time for a substitution, we reckon.

Bring on CICA Blades.

They're the first ever boots with rubber blades instead of studs, angled to let you turn quicker, stop shorter and accelerate faster.

The Blade's flexibility even lets you twist suddenly, without doing the same to your knees.

And, because they spread your weight three times more evenly than studs, you'll still be comfortable when others are feeling the pain.

So now's the time to hang up your old football boots.

And get a pair of CICA Blades.

CICA Blades are available from JJB Sports and other good sports shops. For your nearest stockist call 0800 716245.

Cut corners. Get rid of your studs.

SHARPEN YOUR GAME

CICA *Blades*

A stud's a stud but a blade helps you "turn quicker, stop shorter and accelerate faster", allegedly.

FREE KICK

They can be crazy, solitary, moody or just like Bob Wilson but goalkeepers are usually branded with eccentricities which set them apart. Their kit, often guadier than Gauguin, is yet another affirmation that they are first and foremost specialists. In 1995, Uhlsport ingeniously took this 'unique' factor one step further by including in their range of football boots a model made especially for goalkeepers. The TEMAC No. 1 from Uhlsport has special features: extra cleats, extra spacing between the studs, and a 6mm heel wedge. The result of these innovations – better grip while diving and increased take off reaction. You would think that Tim Flowers of Blackburn and England, who was involved in the development of these boot and actually wears them, needs no further help to propel his headlong rushes out of his area.

own fans want them to be substituted? Kangaroos! If allowed to evolve for another few million years, they'd possibly develop less suitable skin for footwear manufacture, thus averting possible extinction. But for the work of the Kangaroo Protection Co-operative, however, that prospect looks as likely as the next Oz Prime Minister being Rolf Harris.

For many years now kangaroo leather has been used in high-end soccer boots, amongst other products, because it is lightweight, durable and soft. The Kangaroo Protection Co-operative feel enough is enough, and have campaigned vigorously to make consumers aware that kangaroos could be threatened with possible extinction by industry. They feel that, as an indigenous animal, it must be preserved for future generations. Their protection strategy includes persuading supporters to target companies making profit from 'roo leather and to boycott their goods.

This action has led to some manufacturers looking for alternative materials with the same properties as kangaroo leather. The people at Pittards in Irthlingborough, England provide such an alternative, and believe they have developed the finest leather for soccer boots known to man. It is called WR 100 Soccer Plus leather, developed for Puma, and it is treated and moistened with a patented chemical process that penetrates the actual fibres of the leather. When playing in wet conditions, the boots may take on water, but the fibres repel the moisture, so very little is absorbed. This keeps the leather soft and supple. A degree of breathability also means the boots dry out faster than any other leather boots. The unique qualities of Pittard's leather has resulted in Puma switching its top performance shoes form kangaroo to Pittard's leather.

So what's next in boot development and design? We make a few suggestions in the *Extra Time* section after looking further at the 'kangaroo leather crisis'.

SHORT PASS At the launch of the Supreme Cole RS, Reebok placed a £500 bet at 10–1 on Andy Cole ending the 1995/6 season as the Premiership's top scorer. Any winnings will go to the charity Barnados.

Injury time

"IT IS INCUMBENT ON THOSE WHO HAVE CHARGE of the game to see that anything which tends in the smallest degree to increase the ordinary risks of football should not only be thoroughly discouraged but severely dealt with. It is in the interests of football as well as the duty of those who govern it that the tone of the players should be maintained at the highest standard. The game to be played well must be played with a certain amount of spirit, and indeed, without a modicum of excitement a great part of its charm would be gone. But its well-being depends entirely upon a common feeling of fair play and honest work, and no penalty can be too severe for footballers who deviate from such a course, descending to tricks or devices with the object of getting a momentary advantage over an opponent, and evading the unwritten law of fairness which is essential to the maintenance of football as a national sport."

Graham Kelly? Alan Sugar? Alex Ferguson? No, thus wrote C.W. Alcock, president of the F.A. at the time when professionalism was introduced in the 1880s.

Its arrival brought fears of an increase in 'roughness' as football moved, inevitably, away from being just an exercise and amusement, $\longrightarrow$

SHORT PASS Between 30 and 50 professional players retire each year through injury.

81

but the robust nature of football was not a new phenomenon. In its embryonic days, it could be as physical as modern day ice-hockey, with blundering shoulder charges being common-place and boot-inflicted injuries occupational hazards.

An anonymous Etonian, writing in 1831, gives a clear indication of the nature of the sport then;

"I cannot consider the game of football as being at all gentlemanly. It is a game to which the common people of Yorkshire are particularly partial, the tips of their shoes being heavily shod with iron, and frequently death has been known to ensue from the severity of the blows inflicted thereby."

Once football, and in particular the equipment worn by players, became increasingly monitored and regulated, the sort of violence experienced in Yorkshire and elsewhere was effectively reduced, but serious injury could and still did occur. An infamous incident in 1931 showed, tragically, that football still had the potential to be a dangerous sport.

On 5th September, John Thomson, the 22-year old Celtic and Scotland goalkeeper, was killed during a Rangers v Celtic match at Ibrox. The incident which led to his death happened early in the second half. English, the Rangers centre-forward, found himself in a good position near the

Ouch!

One of the most famous players of the early days, the Old Etonian Lord Kinnaird, was well known for hacking. The President of the FA, Sir Francis Marindin, called on Kinnaird's mother one day, and found her worried about her son. "I'm afraid," she said, "that one of these days Arthur will come home with a broken leg." "Never fear, madam," Marindin said. "It will not be his own."

Ouch!

Ian St John remembers the days when it was necessary to hammer studs into the soles of Manfield Hotspurs. The problem was playing on hard ash pitches – the nails would eventually push up through the soles of the boot into your feet and the difficulty was getting the boots off after 90 minutes! That's why old footballers walk funny!

The VEITCH STUDS have been tried by most professional clubs and have been acknowledged by many first-class managers and players as THE PERFECT STUD.
They eliminate all risk of injury to players, caused by protruding nails.
They prevent aching feet, and all jarring, being absolute shock absorbers on hard ground.
They prevent accidents caused by falling on slippery surfaces, they give you perfect balance and will not slip on any surface.

Although these studs were an improvement on nail-protuding ancestors, can any stud claim to "eliminate all risk of injury?"

SHORT PASS Terry Butcher used Nike boots to kick in the dressing room door at Pittodrie after a particularly emotional game between Aberdeen and Rangers.

goal. Thomson ran out to narrow the angle, then, seeing that the situation was desperate, dived at the Rangers player's feet. English shot and Thomson deflected the ball, but he caught the full force of his opponent's boot in his face. He was taken to Victoria Infirmary where a compressed fracture and concussion were diagnosed. His parents were called to his bed-side, and he died a few minutes after they arrived.

Lethal weapons indeed. You can only begin to speculate on the type of self-inflicted injury players might suffer as they lumbered around a field with a ton of leather, lace and metal on the end of each foot. Nails used to secure studs →

Periodically those involved in the game call for a return to high-cut boots to protect the ankle.

Most modern shin pads also offer some form of protection to the ankle area.

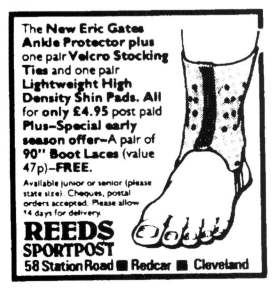
IT'S TIME WE HAD A 'MIDI' BOOT!

—SAYS 'WELL BOSS BOBBY HOWITT

EVERYBODY'S shouting about the new Midi-length fashion these days. Women (tragically) are decidedly in favour, men are not. Except Motherwell boss, Bobby Howitt, that is only it's not skirts he has in mind but football boots!

After seeing about half-a-dozen of his players going down with ankle injuries this season, Bobby would like to see a new Midi boot coming into vogue — a compromise between the old clod-hopper style and the modern slipper style, just to give footballers the much-needed protection.

"We have definitely had an increase of ankle injuries over the seasons," he says. "In our case, this term, we have had JOHN GOLD-THORPE, DAVIE WHITE-FORD, BRIAN HERON and several of the young kids out with this kind of knock.

● BOBBY HOWITT . . .

"Of course it's the boots! They're so flimsy nowadays. I would like to see a return to an extent to what we used to wear. I don't mean the great big things that took you about half a season to break in and then lasted you for the rest of your career, but something with a bigger upper. Maybe about another inch, to take the boot over the ankle bone.

"I mean the boots nowadays lace UNDER the ankle instead of OVER it, which gives no protection and very little support. And even less if the tab at the back of the boot comes off — a player can't even lace them round his ankles.

"So that's what I would like to see. A lightweight boot, but with the upper just about an inch higher so that it could be laced above the ankle bone. But there again, I don't suppose there's much hope of that."

Fortunately, Bobby Howitt's crop of ankle injuries and all the rest seems to have cleared for the moment to reveal a happy situation for him. In terms of players, particularly those up front, he is better off than he has ever been.

"We seem to have more forwards to call on than ever before," he says, "which is all to the good. They are the ones who are so difficult to find nowadays."

Ouch!

George Best was more wary of tackles from the front than sliding tackles from the back which made the crowd wince. "You might end the game with a few bruises on the back of your legs but it was rare to suffer any worse damage because it's actually very difficult deliberately to break a bone with a tackle. With a tackle from the back it's almost impossible because your momentum carries you forward, so cushioning the impact. I was once caught by Johnny Giles, and it could have ended my career. At the start of the game he said to me, "Why can't you be like Bobby Charlton. He's a gentleman". I ignored that. Then, about an hour into the game, he came in over the top. An over-the-top tackle is when a player brings his boot down on the shin bone of his opponent. When done at speed and with enough pressure applied the shin bone breaks. Because we were playing Leeds I was wearing shinguards. If I hadn't been wearing them my leg would most probably have been broken. As it was, Giles' studs tore through my sock, split the shinguard and cut my leg open. And then Giles had the nerve to say to me again; "Why can't you be more like Bobby Charlton?" I was hurt. But I wasn't going to stay down. I wasn't going to let him know that he had hurt me. That would have been belittling myself.

eventually penetrated the sole of the boot, inflicting involuntary acupuncture on the wearer. Studs came off, regularly, and would lie in ambush on the field, waiting patiently for an unsuspecting leg to attach itself to later in the game. And shock absorption? Forget it! 1mm of sodden sock was deemed adequate enough.

So although the old-styled boot offered greater protection in the toe and ankle areas, they posed all sorts of problems for the early player.

The adoption in this country in the 1950s of the 'continental' style of boot, a lightweight model cut low around the ankle, was seen as a major revolution, allowing greater mobility and freeing players from the shackles of the deadweight monstrosities of the past. All was not hunky-dory, however. With the ankle now exposed, players were bound to receive far more knocks in that area, accidental or not, and they discovered too that the new style boots offered less support in the ankle area whilst in motion.

Various devices were examined to give added protection to the ankle area. Ankle protectors, endorsed, surprise surprise by professional

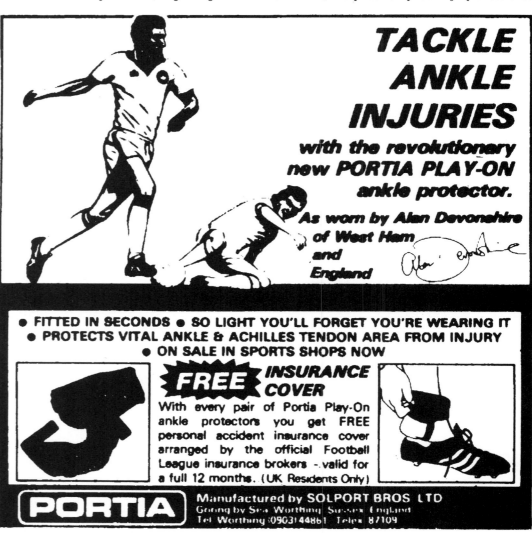

Ankle protection and free insurance cover. What a bargain!

players, such as Alan Devonshire and Eric Gates, came on the market. These offered greater protection to sensitive areas, and could be small, fitting snugly above the boot, or large, reaching up to mid-shin in what looked like a cross between an ankle protector and a shin pad.

Alan Hodson, Assistant Director of Coaching and Education at the FA Medical Centre at Lilleshall, is in no doubt about the effect of modern boots.

"Boots are now lightweight and 'slung-low' under the malleolus of the ankle joint. This gives no support and I am sure has led to an increase in ankle ligament sprains compared to the old type of high laced boot, which offered far more ankle support."

So in support and protection, the modern boot does have its problems.

What about studs? Although the modern alloy studs do wear evenly, they can still break the skin. Whilst Alan Hodson expresses concern that at amateur level, nylon studs which are worn by walking on tarmac or concrete will fray at the edge and cause quite severe cuts to other →

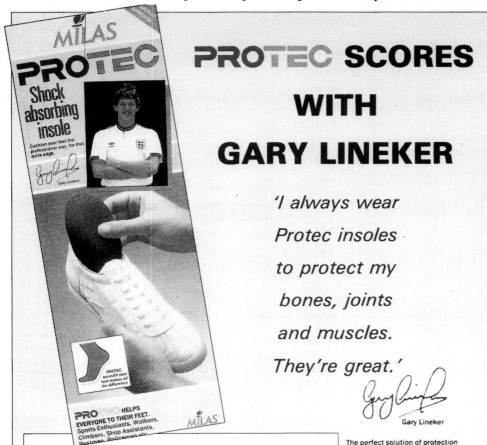
For Gary, one shock absorbing insole did it all.

Shin-guards of every style. Will footballers one day look like ice-hockey players?

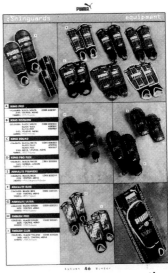

Ouch!

Back in 1967 Dennis Law was having great difficulty convincing people at Old Trafford that there really was something wrong with his right knee. "Some injuries are plainly visible, such as pulled muscles or swollen ankles, but with others there is nothing to see, and that is where the problem arises. I was suffering severe pains in my knee, particularly when I kicked the ball with my right instep, which was something I did most of the time. Rotating the leg to kick in this fashion has the effect of opening the knee joint, and that was where the trouble stemmed from. I would get sharp pains during a game, and then afterwards my knee would stiffen up and become extremely sore. Time and again I was asked to pinpoint the exact source of the pain and then the needle would go in for yet another injection of cortisone. That was supposed to disperse the pain, but it never really worked. Our physiotherapist kept telling me that the problem was in my mind, something I was imagining. I used to ask him; "If it's all in my mind, why don't I get the pain in my head?"

players. On the upside, modern players need no longer fear that they will walk away from their next tackle with their leg looking like a dartboard – the modern screw used to attach the stud is fairly sturdy and less prone to coming off during a game.

Given that between 30 and 50 players retire each year through injury, we still have a long way to go before effectively addressing the problem of the boot-related injury.

Boot manufacturers, god bless them, are forever on the lookout for ways to protect the feet in a search for unique selling points.

For example, Nike's Air Speed D featured an air wedge in the midsole for superior cushioning.

All Patrick boots included the company '35' safe stud system, designed to eliminate uncomfortable stud pressure by using built-in stud inserts which also removed the possibility of studs penetrating the foot.

Quasar claimed to mimic the natural rotation of the foot with their Transfer Plus sole system. Transfer bridges within the system aided and supported the natural movement of the foot, and ensured that support was given to the mid foot area.

New Balance's Saddle in the New Balance SC290 provided lateral support for quick starts and sudden turns, a removable insert moulded to the shape of the foot, as well as incorporating the stud shield to relive cleat pressure.

Football remains a dangerous game and no matter what forms of injury-prevented features are introduced by boot makers, players will still writhe in agony before miraculously recovering and running around like a gazelle.

SHORT PASS To protect players from boot-related injuries, referees were authorised in 1900 to examine a player's boots before a game – a practise still in use today.

Extra time

The Kangaroo Crisis

WHAT WILL BOOTS BE MADE OF IN YEARS TO COME, now that the use of the much-favoured kangaroo leather is being increasingly targeted by irate animal welfare groups? The cry of "Kangaroo taboo? Voodoo!" may well resound through the corridors of power of major boot manufacturers, and less sensitive Australians may call them "a bloody pest" and point in dismay to the buckled roo bars of their 4 wheel drives, but these groups mean business. The whole issue is becoming a real threat to the boot world, and companies may find themselves being forced to look elsewhere for the raw materials for their product.

It may not end there. Despite the fact that modern players appear to be blissfully ignorant of the ecological implications of wearing kangaroo leather, a breed of 'new men' could perhaps emerge in clubs throughout the country; committed vegetarians who refuse to wear leather of any description, will only kick a politically correct ball, and would not thank you for anything other than a salad before a big game.

So what are the options? Realistically, the second scenario of sensitive, caring footballers kitted out in woollen strips and macrame boots, gently caressing a biodegradable plastic ball around the field is just not on. Footballers are footballers, after all, and old habits die hard, so for the foreseeable future let's just leave them with their leather jackets, pre-match steaks and Luther Vandros CDs and look at the alternatives open to boot companies.

Boots made from salmon leather are a possibility; it's soft, durable and smell-free, and →

Did you know that many top-of-the-range football boots are made from Kangaroo leather?

SHORT PASS Ordinary Kangaroo – absorbs almost its own original weight in water; becomes heavy; becomes cold, loses sensitivity of touch. Pittards WR100 Soccer Plus – absorbs little water; remains light; helps retain warmth; retains sensitivity.

would be ideal for the centre-forward who loves to poach in the six-yard box. Having said that, however, it's hard to imagine the concept taking off on a large scale; for some reason these hapless fish do not seem to get animal groups worked up into a lather to the same extent as tuna or dolphins, but what on earth would the studs be made of? Cod roe? And fishing line for laces? Nah…nice idea, but …

There's always crocodile leather, of course, perfect for the inside-left keen to snap up the half chance. 'Puma Gators' does have a certain ring to it. "Anyone seen my Gators?" Yes, this one has distinct potential. Mind you, for the fashion-conscious professional, the heavily textured, glossy appearance of the leather could be a turn-off, and they'd be hell to clean, with all those nooks and crannies harbouring tons of mud. And no doubt it would not be long before angry mobs would take to the streets in protest at the needless slaughter of these cuddly, loveable creatures.

So where does that leave us? After extensive and exhaustive research we feel we may have come up with a solution. Ostrich leather. Ironically enough, the same country which is striving so hard to save its beloved national symbol seems to be at the same time turning a blind eye to the plight of one of its oddest creatures, actively

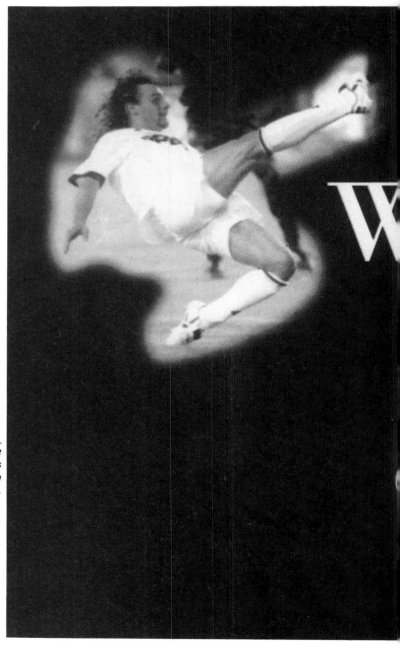

Are white boots on the way back? Valsport's 'White Star', as worn by Marco Simoni.

encouraging the rearing of these beasts for a variety of reasons. This is why we think we are on to a winner, and can but thank the good old Aussies for unwittingly coming up trumps.

Clubs, we feel, should seriously consider keeping a dozen or so of these birds in an enclosure near the ground. As well as providing an added attraction for youngsters before the game ('beat the ostrich' competitions come to mind), a self-generating community of such creatures could ensure that clubs need look no further for a constant supply of leather. It is already used for high quality goods, and rates in the same category as reptile skin, so any excess leather could be sold

to the sad clubs who failed to realise the potential, or made into handbags to be sold in supporters shops, marketed as a peace offering to be made to wives by husbands who have taken six hours to get home from the match.

Who could fail to be convinced, moreover, of the appeal of using ostrich meat in the half time pies? It tastes like veal, is low in fat and cholesterol, and would make a welcome change from the unidentifiable gunge and gristle normally to be found within the crust.

Not convinced? Well how about the cleaners using ostrich feathers to dust the boardroom or, better still, incorporating these fashion →

FREE KICK

An innovation to appear on the soccer field in 1995 was the Reebok Instapump R.S. (removal stud). The boot features a specially designed external chamber that, when inflated, using a hand-held inflater, provides a snug fit. (This inflater would no doubt be kept down a football sock in case of emergencies!) The Instapump weighs in at 8.5ozs., features a K-leather (kangaroo) vamp, cemented sock liner and an R.S. plate with 6 aluminium tipped 'pyramid studs'. Groovy-looking boots, but at £120 per pair surely you would expect to get proper laces!

accessories into their uniforms, replacing the bri-nylon overalls which are normally worn? All that would then be left would be the legs, claws, the neck, and the head, and surely a little ingenuity could quite easily transform these into attractive club backscratchers and banner holders.

And the drawbacks? Admittedly the ostrich leather boots could possibly make the wearer run in a manner akin to watching Duncan Ferguson on speed. Referees may get fed up of censoring strikers who buried their head in the mud after missing a sitter, and players may find it difficult to take off for a high ball, but these disadvantages, when weighed against the obvious benefits to be gained right across the entire operation of the club, are small meat indeed.

What is clear, is that millions of pounds is now being pumped into the research and development of football boots. All manufacturers are searching for new and improved materials for the upper and sole, as well as experimenting with innovative stud and lacing systems.

Synthetic materials for the upper, at present, don't satisfy top players; they prefer soft, supple leather so that they can 'feel' the ball. This prefer-ence is generally imitated by amateur and junior players who follow the lead of the professionals they aspire to be.

The emergence of the Predator and Cica Blades

have challenged our perception of what consti-tutes the perfect boot. The talismatic properties that they promise, along with the interest they've generated, have no doubt encouraged others to develop boots with a difference.

For the masses, football is still a game of dreams. An aspiring youngster can now 'be' the player they idolise – from having his name on the back of an official replica shirt, to wearing the same boots in all but size. If Eric Cantona wears a particular make of boots, you can bet your life thousands of boys will want to wear them too.

In an age where sports-wear is also fashion-wear it makes you wonder what's next. In keeping with the retro-frenzy so popular in soccer, white boots, last witnessed in the seventies, are back on the soccer scene. Marco Simoni of AC Milan wore a pair in the 1995 Champion's League Final.

Blue and red boots are also appearing in some new ranges so it would seem that as we move towards the 21st Century a new attempt is being made to break down the conservative nature of footballers' taste in boots.

Only time will tell whether players performing in the 2002 World Cup will be wearing leather or synthetic boots, black, white or fluorescent boots. Two things are certain though; they'll be paid huge sums of money to wear them and we'll desire to wear their boots, whatever they look like.

SHORT PASS At their factory in Montebeluna, Mizuno check that the day's output of boots aren't defective in any way by choosing a pair from the production line at random, boiling them for four hours and ripping the sole off!

Read all about it!

The boot in literature

THE GAME OF FOOTBALL HAS GENERATED A wealth of literature over the years, covering all aspects of the game. Footballers, many as inarticulate off the pitch as they are on it, never seem to shy away from putting their life-story and deepest thoughts down on paper. With the help of established writers, some of these autobiographies can make relatively interesting reading. Fans too have jumped on the bandwagon, and the fanzine culture shows no signs of abating. Match programmes, with their 'sponsored by' and 'in association with so and so' contents have long since ceased to be a challenging read.

But what about the humble boot? Does this bestudded object of desire warrant mention in the mountain of literature which has been devoted to the beautiful game? Certainly the boot itself has been incorporated into the everyday language of football. On retirement, players do not put their socks 'in the bottom drawer'; they 'hang up their boots.' And when managers buy players to replace a particularly popular team member who has been tempted by the lure of big bucks to try his luck elsewhere, supporters do not debate in hushed tones whether the replacement will be able to 'fit the shorts of the player' who has left – they →

91

wonder instead whether he will be able to 'fill his boots.' Should he fail, moreover, he will be deemed 'not fit enough to tie the laces of' his predecessor.

But the boot in literature? Surprisingly enough, for such an unlikely subject, some top players in this field have felt the need to wax lyrical on its behalf, or at least give it passing mention in their work. The French, famed more for their impassioned treaties on food and wine, are the undoubted league leaders in this championship, in particular one Henri de Montherlant, who not only wrote about boots – he felt moved enough to dedicate a whole poem to them.

Henri was apparently a controversial figure in his day, as much admired as a passionate moralist with a gift for irony and a fine prose style as he was attacked for his arrogant egotism, attitudinising, Fascist leaning, and unwillingness to take on defenders. His early works exalted war and bull-fighting, but his poem, *On Football Boots*, shows a softer, more caring side to the man and goes a long way to redressing the balance. Steady on, Henri, they're only a pair of boots!

Keeping with the French connection, it is a little-known fact that Albert Camus, father of the Existentialist school of philosophy, buddy of Jean Paul Satre and author of such classics as *The Fall* (an early Jurgen Klinsmann biography), was also, in his youth, an accomplished goalkeeper. Contrary to popular belief, this was not due to his ability to prove the non-existence of the ball, or his tendency for luring opposing centre-forwards into lengthy, involved debates on the meaning of life before distracting them with a telling intellectual point just as a high cross came over.

Young Albert played in goal for a university team, RUA, who were based inAlgiers. In a 1957 article in *France Football*, he recalls how his team played scientifically, sportingly and strongly, although unfortunately no mention is made of whether they were any good. The whole experience made such an indelible impression on him that in later life he followed Racing Club de Paris for the sole reason that they wore the same blue and white hooped jerseys as RUA. He probably wore a snorkel parka to the games as well.   →

On Football Boots

Great boots, tip of the young leg, leather scarcely blemished,

Sole thickening of this body which is all weightlessness,

I pull you out of the untidy bag where you've been sleeping beneath muddy shorts:

Referee's whistle in the biting air, pattering soil; I'm pulling out the whole of winter.

Tools of victory between my hands, a little smaller, seen so close,

Lifeless, you who were flying, kicking, at the command of the spirit,

At once tough and childlike, big and small, big and small,

Like him who knows so well the tears which fill his little warrior-eyes!

Still sticky with good oil, still crusted with chunks of earth,

Strong, smoking smell of seaweed, elegance borne of brutality,

With your weight, your scars, your copper hue, the mystery of you,

You're as noble as this earth, and life has not passed you by.

The ankle has shaped you as round as the umbo of a shield.

Kicks have made you supple, you've been moulded into a unique object.

It seems to me that I'd know whom you belonged to, without being told.

My hand, resting on your blocked-toe, is full of gentle respect,

I'm so full of emotion I feel moved to the bottom of my heart.

— *Henri de Montherlant*

The hardest team they faced were Olympic Hussein Dey, whose stadium was situated right beside a cemetery. "They made us realise, without mercy, that there was direct access." he jests, as only French philosophers can.

Olympic's centre-forward was a bloke called Boufarik, nicknamed 'The Watermelon' because of his round appearance and tough green skin, and Camus recalls in graphic detail their crunching encounters; "Boufarik . . . always came down with all his weight right on my kidneys, without counting the cost; Shin massage with football boots, shirt pulled back by the hand, knees in the distinguished parts, and sandwiches against the post . . . in brief, a scourge." Makes Vinnie Jones sound like Mother Theresa. And trust the French to take a packed lunch with them onto the pitch. Before you know it, they'll be inventing slip-on boots.

Back nearer home, in a setting only marginally less prosaic, James Kelman describes going to watch Yoker play Perthshire in his novel *A Disaffection*. "The pitch was particularly muddy on the day in question, allowing full-backs ample scope to practice their mammoth up-enders of

tackles. Player and spectator alike were continually showered with mud as forwards clattered to the ground. One player came in for special attention, and after one bone-shattering tackle the air was filled with the spectators' laughter as they got spattered once again; "There too was the sound of the guy peching when he finally got himself on to his feet and trotted back down the field. You could see the gash down his shin, the blood and the muddy streaks, that special whiteness at the bits where the studs had erased the outer skin."

Lovely. Anyone for a half-time pie?

Boots are given passing mention in many other works, and several authors have shown skill and panache in describing what they are like, and what damage they are capable of inflicting.

John Moynihan depicts an old Victorian footballer named Mr Wrinkle as wearing "a pair of boots which would have winded an elephant", whilst in his article entitled *Sunday Soccer*, amongst the motley crew of misfits who drag their weary, hungover bodies onto the field every Sunday morning are "poets with woollen knickers as bootlaces and intellectuals on motor scooters."

The eponymous hero of Barry Hine's story, *Mr Sugden*, wears boots which "were polished as black and shiny as bombs used by assassins in comic strips." so far, so good, but later on in the same story, Hines devotes a whole paragraph to the noise made by boots and the effect of studs on floor coverings;

"He opened the door and led them down the corridor out into the yard. Some boys waited until he had gone, then they took a run and had a good slide up to the door, rotating slowly as they slid, and finishing up facing the way they had come. Those with rubber studs left long black streaks on the tiles. The plastic and nailed leather studs cut through the veneer and scored deep scratches in the vinyl. When they reached the yard, the pad of the rubber studs on the concrete hardly differed from that in the changing room or the corridor, but the clatter produced by the nailed and plastic studs had a hollow, more metallic ring."

Possibly taking artistic licence a bit too far, aren't we, Barry?

Not to be outdone, Gordon Williams in his story *Stuck In* enlightens us with an insight into the deep and meaningful thoughts racing through the mind of a footballer as he runs onto the pitch.

"You ran out onto the pitch wondering whether your studs were hammered in properly, would a nail come up through your sole, were your laces tied tight enough?"

This appeared in the same year as Barry Hine's effort, so obviously 1968 was a watershed year for classic football boot literature.

Alan Ross attempted to surpass work of this magnitude with his memories of boyhood afternoons at prep school in the autumn term.

"Studs and mud, the memorable dribble, Rhododendrons at the back of the net."

No doubt the Roddy in question was an easy target for the school bullies and spent most of his school years either picking the ball out of the back of the net because he was always forced to play in goals, or picking up the pieces of his glasses which had been smashed by a gang of bounders up to their usual japes and pranks.

One final astonishing fact; an old boot wrote the script for what is widely regarded as being the worst footballing film ever. Jackie Collins was the guilty party, the film being *Yesterday's Hero*, which starred Ian McShane as the heavy- →

drinking wreck of a once great player. Not a lot of people know that!

It is in the comic strips of the '70s and '80s that literature on the football boot received its finest expression. The comic strip which immediately springs to mind, of course, is *Billy's Boots*, which first appeared in the *Scorcher* in 1970, but there were others less well known which played their part as well. Memories are made of this.

Fact met fiction when Roy of the Rovers signed a football boot deal. Yes, when Roy junior emerged to carry on the famous Race name in 1994 it was rumoured that he was in demand by leading boot manufacturers to promote their particular brand.

Apparently Roy's main concern was quality, but not at the expense of the kangaroo population, so many brands were given the boot. It seems he's not only a good football player, but he's ecologically sound as well. After much consideration he plumped for PUMA, who were delighted to have 'Rocky' promote their product.

Why get a fictional character to wear 'real' boots? Easy. He rarely has a bad game, scores 'bootiful' goals, he's a British institution, he ages not, and his every run, tackle and 'Rocket' shot are keenly observed by countless thousands of potential football boot buyers. So what happened to the comic?